The Man Christ Jesus

The Man Christ Jesus

How the Lord Looked, Acted, Prayed, and Loved

by Giacomo Cardinal Biffi

Translated by
Charlotte J. Fasi

SOPHIA INSTITUTE PRESS®
Manchester, New Hampshire

The Man Christ Jesus was originally published in Italian under the title *Gesù di Nazaret. Centro del cosmo e della storia* (Torino: Editrice Elledici, 2000).

Cover design by Theodore Schluenderfritz

On the cover: detail of *The Rich Man Who Went Away Sorrowful*, by Heinrich Hoffmann © SuperStock, Inc. / SuperStock.

Biblical citations are from *The New Jerusalem Bible* (Garden City, New York: Doubleday and Company, Inc., 1985).

Sophia Institute Press®
Box 5284, Manchester, NH 03108
1-800-888-9344
www.sophiainstitute.com

Library of Congress Cataloging-in-Publication Data

Biffi, Giacomo.
   [Gesù di Nazaret. English]
   The man Christ Jesus : how the Lord looked, acted, prayed, and loved / Giacomo Cardinal Biffi ; translated by Charlotte J. Fasi.
     p. cm.
   ISBN 978-1-933184-39-5 (pbk. : alk. paper) 1. Jesus Christ — Person and offices. I. Title.
   BT203.B53313 2008
   232 — dc22

                           2008043845

Contents

Part One
The Man Christ Jesus
According to Those Who Knew Him

1. Christ's Physical Appearance

2. Christ's Personality

3. Christ's Originality

Part Two
The Man Christ Jesus by the Light of Faith

4. Christ the Son of God

Biographical note: Giacomo Cardinal Biffi 121

Such a one will receive blessing from Yahweh,
Saving justice from the God of salvation.
Such is the people that seeks him,
that seeks the God of Jacob.

Psalm 24:5-6

Egli otterrà benedizione dal Signore,
giustizia da Dio sua salvezza.
Ecco la generazione che lo cerca,
che cerca il tuo volto, Dio di Giacobbe.

Salmo 23 (24), 56

Preface

While they were reading this book to me, two texts continually came to mind: the prologue of Luke's Gospel and the beginning of the first letter of John. The more they read, the more it became clear to me that these two texts were a perfect summary of this wonderful book.

Cardinal Giacomo Biffi addresses our wish to know the truth about Jesus of Nazareth. Through careful attention to the evangelical texts, he gives us a clearer and more vivid image of the Son of God's humanity during his mortal life. It is the testimony of one with a long and intimate acquaintance with the writings of the Evangelists. As a result, he has insight into Jesus the man.

With exceptional authority, the apostle John tells us what he learned being with Jesus. He was a man. John saw him and heard his voice. In his Gospel, he recalls his own experience living with the Man of Nazareth. He was

The Man Christ Jesus

a witness to his transfiguration and even followed him to his death at Calvary.

Luke, in his prologue, tells of the care he took collecting news of Jesus from those who had seen this Nazarene. They were eyewitnesses to the events in his life. It was written with the love of a disciple who couldn't leave out a single recollection of Jesus. John's experience is direct. He was one of the Twelve. He followed Jesus from the beginning of his ministry.

The author of this book, with the same care and love, takes from the evangelists each bit of information about Jesus' life: each word, each gesture, his physical appearance, his sentiments, his thoughts, and his will. A portrait of an extraordinary man emerges from this examination. It stirs in the reader a desire to learn, *who is Jesus?*

Cardinal Biffi wishes to bring alive the human and divine figure of Christ. The often-referenced evangelical text he continually cites allows him to inform today's world about Christ as described by the apostles in the time of the Roman dominance. The author presents the witness of the apostles with nearly the same authority as the evangelists. He does so in a contemporary style never diverging from the inspired books.

I must confess that I have been won over by the beauty of this presentation of Jesus. Often, some detail of his life or physical appearance reveals to us the complexity of this human figure. Here, with total clarity, the figure of Christ is made known to the reader. Only his voice is missing from this examination of Jesus. He speaks in the open air to thousands of people; they all listen. His words move them. To hear Christ speak, men leave their work and women their homes. The author records this power by stressing the vigor and physical health of our Lord. It was because the author knew how to collect and put together all the facts scattered throughout the New Testament that he was able to create a profile of Jesus.

The presence of Christ throughout this book is not an end in itself. Rather, the greatness of Jesus inspires us to know him better. Research helps us understand the mystery and vision of this man. With great clarity and intelligence, this book achieves it. I can say in complete honesty that it is one of the greatest books of our times. It is truly the highest testimonial that today's Church gives to its Divine Founder. Each century God has a need to renew and update the apostolic witness. This text is the testimonial and confession of faith that the Church gives to today's generations.

The Man Christ Jesus

The first part of the book describes the external aspects of Jesus. It examines his psychology and originality. In the second part, the author discusses in greater detail, *who is Jesus?* This is his approach to the mystery. The first three chapters lay the foundation for understanding the unique greatness of Christ. As St. Leo the Great[1] said, "Each day Peter confesses: You are the Christ, the Son of the living God." This confession makes up the last part of the book. Penetrating the mystery of Christ with reason and a secular approach is contrasted with the confession of Peter and Church teaching.

Cardinal Biffi could not have given us a greater gift than this solemn confession of faith. It is a faith unchangeable but renewable in time for as long as man is alive. This confession, not adding anything to the greatness of Christ, is the rock on which every hope, certainty, and the Church itself was founded. We wish to hear this confession repeated from those who continue the mission of the apostles. They have received the mandate of confirming the faith in believers.

Who, then, is Christ? According to the apostles, he is the Son of the living God and the Savior of the world. He is the Head, the only Son of God, and the sum of all things.

---

[1] St. Leo the Great (d. 461), Pope from 440-461.

Preface

If the greatness of Christ exalts us in his mission as Savior, it is still nearly unimaginable for even true Christians to have enough faith to recognize God's presence among us as our brother, united to us by the love of God himself.

Paul wrote to the Colossians the glorious hymn on Christ's purpose in God's design. Although less exalting, John's Gospel goes beyond the same mission of the Word incarnate. John reaches deeply into the mystery of God himself. All that Christ is in relationship to man and to the created universe is surpassed by the teaching of the fourth Gospel on the divinity of Jesus. Under the sign of humility, the Word of God is made present and given to man: "God has so loved the world that he gave his only begotten Son."[2]

The second part of the book responds directly to our need to know who the Master of Nazareth is. But the greatness of Jesus transcends every human insight. Nothing we find out is enough. Human intelligence cannot reveal the mystery of Jesus. It is the same Christ who asks his own — who for him have abandoned everything — what they think of their Master. The answer, in Jesus' words, requires God himself to reveal the mystery of who he is in the person of Jesus.

[2] Cf. John 3:16.

The Man Christ Jesus

The last part of the book is a summary of the passages from Matthew, chapter 16, and verses beginning with twelve. Jesus is in the territory of Caesarea Philippi and asks, "Who do the people say is the Son of man?" People are uncertain. This is contrasted with the clear and solemn declaration of Peter. The people, asking themselves who Jesus of Nazareth was, were confused. They did not have faith. And only faith could reveal Christ's nature to the disciples. Jesus remains an enigma for them. They had an opinion about Him. But whenever they spoke, their thoughts about Jesus were confused. This is contrasted to the confession of Peter.

The Man Christ Jesus brings to life this confession of faith. Its greatness and strength cannot be ignored. We realize that it is not just any writer who speaks, but the Church itself proclaiming its faith to the world. This book has the explosive force of a confession. It rejects and condemns any judgment that reduces Christ to mere human greatness. God is brought to life in Jesus.

Don Divo Barsotti
Casa San Sergio, Settignano (Tuscany)
March 25, 2000

≈

In Search of the Human Face of Christ

Jesus is a unique event. No one is more historically important than Jesus of Nazareth.

Whoever calls himself a Christian in the most impassioned sense of the term, knows, believes, and proclaims that Jesus is the only true Master. He is the only true Savior of everyone, the vital Head of a redeemed and renewed humanity, the first born of the Father who gives us the "power to become sons of God."[3]

Therefore, it is a believer's duty to grow in knowledge of him. It is a gratifying and endless task.

The intent of this inquiry is to draw people closer to Jesus of Nazareth. Like those who were with him during his life on earth, we shall first focus on his human side by revealing his personality and character. (The second

[3] Cf. John 1:12.

part is theological and assumes faith on the part of the reader.)

Through our investigation, we will attempt to reach a more detailed understanding of Jesus. To improve our fellowship with Christ, our preliminary research should be thorough and unrestrained.

We have no photographs, portraits, voice recordings of Christ, or manuscripts written by him. We do have eloquently phrased and specific information: his words, the testimony of those who were with him and the historical dates surrounding him.

These precious resources have been gathered, organized, compared, and contrasted. The image of Jesus created from them is accurate and truthful.

⤳

To clarify our intention, we have borrowed what police use throughout the world: the idea of a "composite profile." In it, for lack of better evidence, the physical features of a suspect are reconstructed based on recollections and other information police receive from witnesses.

Using a composite profile is a bold and unusual approach. Some might even call it irreverent. But perhaps Jesus would pardon our audacity. Even he compared himself to an outlaw when describing his final coming like the surprise of a thief in the night.[4]

In the clearest sense of the word, we pursue the "fugitive" Lord. We do so because our desire to see Jesus is integral to our faith. We pursue him because of our hope to fully and openly embrace Christ. We pursue him out of love. Like every true love, it suffers being alone and wishes to have loved ones nearer.

As in our case, a composite profile is an approximate reconstruction. Even the human truth about the Son of God exceeds what we know about his identification.

After completing our work of bringing to life the "humanness" of Christ — his temperament, his qualities as a man, and the richness of his personality — our need to know him will still not be satisfied. To the contrary, it will increase our desire and eagerness to meet Jesus face-to-face and see him with our own eyes.

⤳

The accuracy and value of a profile depend upon the truthfulness of the witnesses. Here, fortunately, we are lucky. As believers, we can count on divinely inspired

[4] Cf. Matt. 24:42-44.

testimony. We must never forget this fact while remaining aware that the writings of the sacred texts must be accurately examined with the help of historical and literary controls.

Even when studied by human authority, the evangelical narrations are excellent resources for the honest researcher.

The objections raised by scientific or secular critics usually come from not admitting God's direct intervention in human events. Therefore, the present inquiry will stay within the natural world. Still, we hope the results of our investigation will be largely acceptable to those without faith.

⁓

Even today, many try to imagine the thoughts, ideas, intentions, and tastes of Jesus Christ. This proves he continues to cast a spell over us. Assuming no one speaks falsely about Jesus — a frequently occurring temptation — knowing him better is the greatest experience we can have.

Besides reading the Gospels, there are no cultural and correct ways of learning the truth about Christ. The other possible sources are either silent (which is the case of the non-Christian writings) or lack credibility (which is the case with the prophetic gospels). Therefore, one either believes the Gospels or never mentions Christ. It serves no purpose to make up stories.

For our part, we promise that the Gospels will back up everything presented here.

We hope this complete and unbiased reading of the sacred texts leads to a greater understanding of Jesus.

The Man Christ Jesus

Part One

The Man Christ Jesus
According to Those Who Knew Him

≈

Chapter One

Christ's Physical Appearance

We begin with what was most notable and appealing in the figure of Christ. Anyone seeing him on the streets of Palestine immediately recognized these qualities.

Style of dress

How does Jesus of Nazareth dress? Contrary to beliefs, we must say he dresses very well.

His look, in his appearance and lifestyle, is quite different from that of John the Baptist, to whom he is compared.[5] Jesus dresses like observant Israelites and prominent Jews who, in deference to prescribed law,[6] adorn the edges of their cloaks with colored tassels. Jesus criticizes the vanity of the Pharisees and scribes for unduly elongating their

[5] Cf. Matt. 11:18-19.
[6] Cf. Num. 15:38; Deut. 22:12.

tasseled trim.[7] His style of clothing is illustrated by the episode of the woman hoping to stop her bleeding by touching one of these tassels: "Then suddenly from behind came a woman, who had been suffering from a hemorrhage for twelve years, and she touched the fringe of his cloak, for she was thinking, 'If only I can touch his cloak I shall be saved.' "[8]

The tunic he wears is not simply made. It is seamlessly woven in one piece. Under the Cross, the soldiers draw lots for it. Cutting the cloth would lessen its worth: "Let's throw dice to see who is to have it."[9]

Refinement and authority

Appearance is not limited to clothing. Jesus has refined and assured manners. Like the centurion from Capernaum and the Canaanite woman, even approaching strangers respectfully call him "lord."[10]

Little by little, as Christ's teaching becomes known, the title of "master" is given to him more often. Even his

[7] Cf. Matt. 23:5.
[8] Cf. Matt. 9:20-21.
[9] Cf. John 19:23-24.
[10] Cf. Matt. 8:6-8; 15:22-28.

enemies, the Pharisees, the Sadducees, and the doctors of the law, call him master.[11]

People of the highest social order invite this distinguished man into their houses. The more notable Pharisees and the wealthy but despised tax collectors repeatedly host him at dinners.[12] This scandalizes those believing themselves righteous.

Jesus is recognized as master. This allows him to explain the word of God at Saturday gatherings in the synagogues at Capernaum and Nazareth.[13] He never rejects these titles of respect. Indeed, he accepts them: "You call me Master and Lord and rightly; so I am."[14]

Social life

How can we describe the followers of Jesus? He certainly excludes no one from this group. The settings of his parables show that they are mostly shepherds, fishermen, peasant farmers, and laborers. But scribes, Pharisees, and other cultured men also are there.

[11] Cf. Matt. 22:16, 24, 36.

[12] Cf. Matt. 9:10; Luke 5:29; 7:36-50; 11:37; 14:1; 15:1-2.

[13] Cf. Mark 1:21-22; 6:2.

[14] John 13:13.

The Man Christ Jesus

If he has a preference, it is for the humble and unfortunate: "Come to me, all you who labor and are overburdened, and I will give you rest."[15] But he repudiates neither the heads of synagogues nor the Roman centurions.

He preaches that the educated classes have no advantage in learning important things: "At that time, Jesus exclaimed, 'I bless you, Father, Lord of heaven and of earth, for hiding these things from the learned and the clever and revealing them to little children.' "[16] But he does not think it a waste of time to have long and nightly discussions with a teacher of Israel such as Nicodemus.[17]

In the same way, he says that the rich are at a disadvantage in gaining salvation. In contrast, the poor are particularly blessed. For them, the kingdom of heaven is more easily reached.[18]

But he also states that no one should despair. Everything is possible with God, even a camel passing through the eye of a needle.[19]

[15] Matt. 11:28.
[16] Matt. 11:25.
[17] Cf. John 3:1-21.
[18] Cf. Matt. 19:23-26; Luke 6:20-25.
[19] Cf. Matt. 19:26.

Christ's Physical Appearance

On the other hand, while Jesus remains on good terms with the poor, he still has many close relationships with well-to-do people. Among the most prominent are: Joseph of Arimathea, "a rich man";[20] the proprietor of the room of the last supper ("He will show you a large upper room furnished with couches, all prepared. Make the preparations for us there");[21] Johanna, the wife of Herod's steward Chuza;[22] and the family in Bethany, where Mary smashes a precious alabaster vase containing a perfume valued, by an expert like Judas, at three hundred denariis. For love of Jesus she coolly breaks the pot, anointing him with its oil.[23]

The "houses" of Jesus

Some wealthy patrons let Jesus use their homes as bases for his traveling ministry. They could afford to host him. The saying: "Foxes have holes and the birds of the air have nests, but the Son of Man has nowhere to lay his head"[24]

[20] Matt. 27:57.
[21] Mark 14:15.
[22] Cf. Luke 8:3.
[23] Cf. John 12:3-5.
[24] Matt. 8:20.

must be understood in context. Its objective is to warn anyone wishing to join him that Christ's mission makes it impossible for him and his followers to live secure and stable lives. Taken to the letter, this would be denied by all the Gospels.

In Galilee, his usual domicile is Peter's house.[25] From here, he sets out to preach in nearby villages. But upon his return, at the end of the journey, a crowd awaits him: "When he returned to Capernaum, some time later, word went around that he was in the house, and so many people collected that there was no room left, even in front of the door."[26]

But hints about a place to live, although temporary, are frequent: "He went home again, and once more such a crowd collected . . ."[27]

Within the comfort of four walls, he explains to his disciples what he said in the open to all people: "When he had gone into the house, away from the crowd, his disciples questioned him about the parable."[28]

[25] Cf. Mark 1:29-35.
[26] Mark 2:1-2.
[27] Mark 3:20.
[28] Mark 7:17.

He discreetly responds to all their questions, both practical and personal: "When he had gone indoors and they were by themselves his disciples asked him 'Why were we unable to drive it out?' "[29]

Even abroad in Phoenicia, he finds refuge under a roof: "He left that place and set out for the territory of Tyre. There he went into a house and did not want anyone to know he was there; but he could not pass unrecognized."[30]

At Bethany, near Jerusalem, Jesus gets warm and rested in a friendly place. It is the house of Martha and Mary, setting of the beautiful scene described by Luke[31] and where Jesus goes to spend the nights in the last days before his arrest and death.

The vigor and good health of the Lord

Throughout the narrations, Jesus seems in good health and physically active. He is seldom tired.

He loves to begin his day early: "In the morning, long before dawn, he got up and left the house and went off to a lonely place and prayed there."[32]

[29] Cf. Mark 9:28.

[30] Mark 7:24.

[31] Luke 10:38-42.

[32] Mark 1:35.

On important occasions, he takes long prayer vigils: "Now it happened in those days, that he went onto the mountain to pray; and he spent the whole night in prayer to God. When he came down, he summoned his disciples and picked out twelve of them; he called them apostles."[33]

He supports an exhausting range of activities, Mark notes repeatedly: "There were so many coming and going that there was no time for them even to eat."[34]

His workdays are hectic. Many people come and go until late at night: the sick looking for relief, truth-seekers asking to hear him and theological foes engaging him in grueling debates.

When he leaves for some air, they quickly catch him: "Simon and his companions set out in search of him. When they found him they said, 'Everybody is looking for you.' "[35]

Jesus takes long walks. Yet, he tires as noted in the Gospel of John: "Jacob's well was there, and Jesus, tired by the journey [that had taken him from Judea to Samaria],

[33] Luke 6:12-13.
[34] Cf. Mark 3:20; 6:31.
[35] Cf. Mark 1:36-37.

sat down by the well."[36] His ministry is a continuous pilgrimage from Palestine to Caesarea Philippi and the territories of Tyre and Sidon.

His last journey, a steep hike from Jericho to Jerusalem has been described as a great accomplishment: "Under the blazing sun on unshaded paths across massive rock formations, in the desert, he had to complete a march which included a six-hour climb: He overcame variations in levels of more than a thousand meters."[37]

Physical beauty

Was Jesus handsome or ugly? Surprisingly, it was hotly debated in the early centuries of Christianity. Opposing sides argued their positions solely on ideology. However, nothing was accomplished.

The sacred books never mentioned how Jesus looked. Nevertheless, an episode in the Gospel of Luke gives us some insight:

It happened while he was speaking, a woman in the crowd raised her voice and said, "Blessed the womb

[36] Cf. John 4:6.

[37] Karl Adam, *Jesus the Christ* (Brescia, 1944), 88.

that bore you and the breasts that fed you!" But he replied, "More blessed still are those who hear the word of God and keep it!"[38]

The unknown admirer cannot control her passion for Jesus. She even interrupts him. This passage gives us some indication of Jesus' charm and beauty. We infer this from the physical nature of the praise. Above all, the Lord's response makes the word of God more relevant.

The eyes

Although physical in nature, an element of human beauty closely reflects the soul: it is the splendor of the eyes. The Master himself notes it: "The lamp of the body is the eye. It follows that if your eyes are clear your whole body will be filled with light."[39]

The eyes of Jesus had to be enchanting, penetrating, and dazzlingly magnetic. Those who saw them could never forget them. This explains how frequently the Evangelists (and in particular Mark, who refers to the recollections of Peter) emphasize his looks.

[38] Luke 11:27-28.
[39] Matt. 6:22.

It is important to catch shades of meaning in the original texts. The verb "to look" is used in three expressive variations: "to look around," "to look on high," and "to look within."

• *The look around:* When Jesus looks around, he silences, frightens, and charms people at the same time. Before he begins preaching, his gaze attracts the crowd's attention.[40] With this look he expresses the love and concern he has for his disciples: "And looking at those sitting in a circle round him, he said, 'Here are my mother and my brothers.' "[41] With this look he opens up hearts to his teaching: "Jesus looked around and said to his disciples, 'How hard it is for those who have riches to enter the kingdom of God . . . It is easier for a camel to pass through the eye of a needle than for someone rich to enter the kingdom of God.' "[42]

At times, it is a mute glance intensely conveying a clear message: "And when he had surveyed it all, as it was late by now, he went to Bethany with the Twelve."[43]

---

[40] Cf. Luke 6:20.

[41] Mark 3:34.

[42] Cf. Mark 10:23-25.

[43] Cf. Mark 11:11.

The Man Christ Jesus

At other times, it is a look so filled with pain and contempt that his audience falls silent. They dare not speak: "Then he looked angrily round at them, grieved to find them so obstinate, and said to the man, 'Stretch out your hand.' "[44]

• *The look on high:* So that he might be heard, Christ looks up to heaven in an impassioned prayer to the Father.[45] But he also looks up to search for a smiling face in the foliage. To see more clearly, a senior tax collector had perched like a street urchin on the branches of a sycamore tree: "When Jesus reached the spot, he looked up and spoke to him: 'Zaccheus, come down. Hurry, because I am to stay at your house today.' "[46]

• *The look within:* However, his eyes are most impressive when he looks inside people, nearly seeing into their hearts.

As in the case of Mark 10:27, he does this when communicating some important truth to his listeners. "Jesus gazed at them and said, 'By human resources it is impossible, but not for God: because for God everything is possible.' "

[44] Mark 3:5.
[45] Cf. Mark 6:41; 7:34.
[46] Luke 19:5.

And again in the case of Luke 20:17-18: "But he looked hard at them and said . . . 'Anyone who falls on that stone [the cornerstone, i.e., the Messiah, Son of God] will be dashed to pieces; anyone it falls on will be crushed.' "

However, standing before the rich man living an innocent life, asking for eternal life, the Gospel notes: "Jesus looked steadily at him and was filled with love for him."[47]

The apostle Peter's existence is forever marked by two transforming glances. In the first encounter, "Jesus looked at him and said, 'You are Simon, son of John; you shall be called Cephas, which means rock.' "[48] And in the hour of his betrayal, "the Lord turned and looked straight at Peter, and Peter . . . went outside and wept bitterly."[49]

≈

Obviously, we could go on highlighting every detail found in the Gospels. Collecting every word helps us understand how Jesus appeared to those he met on the streets of Palestine.

[47] Mark 10:21.
[48] John 1:42.
[49] Luke 22:61-62.

The Man Christ Jesus

However, at this point, the human figure of Christ is beginning to be revealed. This encourages us to explore deeper. We shall now attempt to build a psychological profile of our Savior.

≈

Chapter Two

Christ's Personality

A person's interior life is somewhat mysterious. Even more difficult is our attempt to know the richness of Christ's soul and to understand his thoughts. Although emotional and difficult, it is necessary and fascinating research. We do it humbly, knowing the inadequacy of our thinking. The Evangelists help us in our task. Through them, our Savior openly reveals himself. In scattered testimony, often second-hand and casual in nature, we discover his thoughts, his mentality, his affections, his sentiments, his temperament, his words, and his manner.

Clarity of ideas

What chiefly strikes us in Jesus' role as educator is the clarity of his ideas. Everything is precisely stated. There are no doubts or uncertainties. Indecision, biases, and conditional phrases are never found in his speeches. He never uses the flowery or seductive language used to express weak ideas.

Indeed, Jesus speaks confidently. It would bother us if we were not moved by the insight and enlightenment of his teaching.

In all the arguments used, the vision of Christ remains intact. There is no fragmentation or incoherence. Rather, there are two fundamental and recurring themes: that of the "Father," who is at the beginning of every life, and that of the "Kingdom," the source and goal of our restless longing and pilgrimage through history.

Attention to human reality

Jesus is not so lost in meditation that he loses sight of the little things. Nor is there proof he is a superhuman uninvolved in ordinary events. To the contrary, Jesus is an attentive observer. Indeed, he is interested in the everyday activities we all perform.

His comments and parables are daily-life observations, both then and now. Among them are: the baby fussing to be fed; children playing outside while listening to traditional nonsense rhymes; the annoying neighbor bothering you at night until you answer him; the woman not leaving until she finds the money that rolled under the furniture; the suffering woman giving birth, whose pain is replaced with joy when she sees the baby born to her; the servants goofing off while the master is away; the dishonest and cunning administrator; the confusion of a wedding feast; the bankers who charge interest on capital; the thief who breaks into the house without warning; the traveler who runs into bandits; the unemployed workers waiting to be hired; the housewife kneading dough and leaving it to rise. And much more.

No one speaking this way is aloof and wrapped up in himself. Rather, Jesus is interested in taking part in the human comedy. The most humbling things are used as examples: the washing of dishes, the lamp and the lampstand, the salt for use in the kitchen, the glass of fresh water, the old wine better than the new, the tattered vestment, the speck and the beam, the eye of the needle, the damage caused by moths and mildew, the short-lived flowers of the field, the first leaves of the fig tree, the mustard tree, the seed that falls to the earth, the fisherman's net that catches both edible fish and ones to throw back, the wandering sheep lost from the flock. This list goes on. At this point we should be convinced that Jesus cannot be compared to the grand theoretician who doesn't see the problems of ordinary people.

The Man Christ Jesus

Christ has feelings for simple things and knows how to use them to make his points. He tells even the simplest people the greatest truths. Jesus talks clearly about new ideas. This is very different from today's intellectuals doing most of the public speaking.

Strong will

Jesus combines a brilliant mind and effective speech with a strong will. He makes rapid decisions and easily grasps truths. Christ embraces his mission with such love that he cannot be distracted.

At times, the apostles record how determined Jesus can be.

We note two examples: "Now it happened that as the time drew near for him to be taken up, he resolutely turned his face toward Jerusalem."[50] The original text is even more significant: "He stiffened his countenance in order to go in the direction of Jerusalem."

Jesus is a leader. Throughout his travels, he goes ahead of all the others. At times, on planned journeys, he shows such resolve that he strikes fear in those around him: "They were on the road, going to Jerusalem. Jesus was

[50] Luke 9:51.

walking on ahead of them: they were in a daze, and those who followed were apprehensive."[51]

Liberty before his relatives and critics

Jesus is always shown as a man moving freely. No one stops him from completing his work.

He is free from his "clan" who think him mad.[52] He is free before the leaders of his people and those opposing his ministry. Standing before them, he dryly responds: "My Father still goes on working, and I am at work, too."[53]

Although he recognizes and respects authority, he doesn't fear influential people. As an example, Jesus feels contempt for the Pharisees and scribes, among others.[54] He strongly criticizes the Sadducees occupying the highest priestly offices: "You are wrong, because you understand neither the scriptures nor the power of God."[55] He has no compliments for Herod, the tetrarch of Galilee:

[51] Mark 10:32.
[52] Cf. Mark 3:21.
[53] John 5:17.
[54] Cf. Matt. 23:1-32.
[55] Matt. 22:29.

The Man Christ Jesus

"You may go and give that fox this message: 'Look! Today and tomorrow I drive out devils . . .'"[56]

On the other hand, his frankness is also recognized by those hostile to him, such as the Pharisees and the Herodians who once addressed him this way: "Master, we know that you are an honest man, that you are not afraid of anyone, because human rank means nothing to you, and that you teach the way of God in all honesty."[57]

Freedom from friends

He is free — something more difficult — from his friends when they keep him from his mission.

One classic and striking example involves the apostle Peter. First, out of respect, he is praised at Caesarea Philippi for his inspired profession of faith. But immediately after denying his Master the way of the cross, Peter is attacked in the harshest language:

Then, taking him aside, Peter started to rebuke him. "Heaven preserve you, Lord," he said. "This must not happen to you." But he turned and said to

[56] Cf. Luke 13:32.
[57] Matt. 22:16.

Peter, "Get behind me, Satan! You are an obstacle in my path, because you are thinking not as God thinks but as human beings do."[58]

In a time of crisis, Jesus does not back down even when forsaken by most of the disciples. His offering up "flesh" and "blood" as food and drink troubles them. But he does not stop being controversial to make it easier for them to accept him. It would be dishonest: "Jesus said to the twelve: 'Do you also wish to leave?' "[59] This is one of the most dramatic and unforgettable phrases ever spoken by our Savior.

Freedom from the judgments of others

Jesus is also free from the "appearance of virtue." This means he never worries about the hateful and baseless things people say about him. He goes his own way despite the harm to his reputation: "The son of man came, eating and drinking, and they say, 'Look, a glutton and a drunkard, a friend of tax collectors and sinners.' "[60]

[58] Matt. 16:22-23.
[59] Cf. John 6:67.
[60] Matt. 11:19.

The Man Christ Jesus

His warning to others was a warning to himself: "Alas for you when everyone speaks well of you!"[61]

Sensibility of the spirit

It often happens that an independent and freed soul is cold, indifferent, and unaware of the hardship of others. It is not so with Jesus. His soul endows him with strong feelings and a sensibility for all people.

An example is the episode of the man with the withered hand. Jesus is so angry that he uses the unfortunate person to make a theological point. "And they were watching him to see if he would cure him on the Sabbath day, hoping for something to charge him with."[62] He asks the impaired man to rise and stand in the middle of the crowd. Then, according to the original text, Jesus looked angrily at those present. He was saddened by the hardness of their hearts.

Heartfelt compassion

The apostles frequently note the compassion Jesus feels for all human miseries. They use a word evoking a

[61] Cf. Luke 6:26.
[62] Cf. Mark 3:1-6.

physical emotion: *(splagchnizesthai)*, meaning to feel compassion and referring to internal organs *(splagchna)* and the innermost feelings of the heart.

It is this spiritual nature that prevails when the Savior hears the heartfelt cry of the two blind men from Jericho: "Jesus felt pity for them";[63] on seeing the anguish of the mother who follows the funeral of her young and only son, "When the Lord saw her he felt sorry for her and said to her, 'Don't cry!' ";[64] in taking notice that there is a hungry crowd, "I feel sorry for all these people; they have been with me three days now and have nothing to eat";[65] and thinking about a scattered and leaderless throng, "he saw a large crowd and he took pity on them because they were like sheep without a shepherd."[66]

Friendship

Jesus makes friends with many people. He is particularly close to some. Christ calls the apostles his friends.[67] It

[63] Matt. 20:34.
[64] Luke 7:13.
[65] Mark 8:1.
[66] Mark 6:34.
[67] Cf. John 15:5.

is a close and caring friendship. He worries about their becoming tired: "Come away to some lonely place all by yourselves and rest for a while."[68] Among the Twelve, he feels closest to Peter, James, and John. He wants them near him in the majestic hour of the Transfiguration[69] and in his most painful hour at Gethsemane.[70] "The disciple Jesus loves" is attributed to John alone.[71]

Beyond his apostolic circle, Jesus felt great affection for members of the family at Bethany: "Jesus loved Martha and her sister and Lazarus."[72]

Women and children

Jesus' fondness for children is noted: "People were bringing little children for him to touch them. The disciples scolded them, but when Jesus saw this he was indignant [literally: 'he could not tolerate'], and he said to them, 'Let the little children come to me; do not stop them; for it is to such as these that the kingdom of God

---

[68] Mark 6:31.

[69] Cf. Mark 9:2-8.

[70] Cf. Mark 14:32-42.

[71] Cf. John 13:23; 19:26; 20:2; 21:7-20.

[72] John 11:5.

belongs . . .' Then he embraced them, laid his hands on them, and gave them his blessing."[73]

He shows gentleness toward women and often defends them. He saves from stoning the unknown woman caught in adultery.[74] During a banquet he is invited to by a Pharisee, Jesus praises the daring sinner who, despite protests from the master of the house, anoints him with perfume and bathes him with her tears.[75] He responds angrily to Judas and the other table companions criticizing Mary, the sister of Lazarus, for her unexpected humility: "Leave her alone. Why are you upsetting her? What she has done for me is a good work."[76]

Tears and joy

Jesus is exceptionally strong and poised. He is also calm and fearless in a storm that could sink the boat he and his apostles are traveling in.[77] Similarly, with an imposing spirit he confronts and charms the angry crowd

---

[73] Mark 10:13-16.

[74] Cf. John 8:1-11.

[75] Cf. Luke 7:36-50.

[76] Cf. Mark 14:6.

[77] Cf. Mark 4:35-41.

from Nazareth threatening to kill him: "When they heard this, everyone in the synagogue was enraged. They sprang to their feet and hustled him out of town. They took him up to the top of the hill overlooking their town and intended to throw him off the cliff, but he passed straight through the crowd and walked away."[78]

He is not, however, an unflappable gentleman of the Victorian society who as a point of honor never shows his emotions. To the contrary, Jesus is often upset, such as when he finds Mary, the sister of Lazarus, crying: "At the sight of her tears . . . Jesus was greatly distressed."[79] At the thought of the death of his friend Lazarus he was brought to tears, so much so that those present commented, "See how much he loved him."[80]

While approaching Jerusalem from the hills and contemplating its destruction, he cannot hold back his tears: "As he drew near and came in sight of the city, he shed tears over it and said, 'If you, too, had only recognized on this day the way to peace!'"[81]

[78] Cf. Luke 4:28-30.
[79] Cf. John 11:33.
[80] Cf. John 11:35-36.
[81] Cf. Luke 19:41-42.

But Jesus also can be excited, as he is with the disciples rejoicing at the completion of their first evangelical mission: "Just at this time, filled with joy by the Holy Spirit, he said, 'I bless you, Father, Lord of Heaven and earth . . ."[82]

Jesus is a man who can cry and be happy. Jesus crying is well documented. His joy can be inferred. The fun-loving publicans welcome him at their table. It is clear from this that he knows how to be happy with his companions.

When around overworked and exhausted people, he gives them strength. But he does not ruin the fun of a banquet with unsuitable remarks or warnings about world hunger.

Keeping to the Lord's example, St. Paul affirms the golden rule of conduct: "Rejoice with others when they rejoice, and be sad with those in sorrow."[83]

The Jewishness of Jesus

A person might believe that Christ's superior humanity and enlightenment surpasses any human, ethnic, or cultural classification. Lacking the cultural and civic ties

[82] Cf. Luke 10:17-21.

[83] Rom. 12:15.

of belonging to a state, he is nearly a man without one. But we would be wrong in thinking that way.

Jesus reasons, speaks and acts like a son of Israel. His "Jewishness" is unquestioned. Anyone not accepting this could never know the truth. His understanding of Jesus would be false.

Christ's outlook, thought process, and Nazarene speech patterns are typical of his people. He frequently cites biblical citations. The names of the most noted and dearest of his compatriots — Abraham, Moses, David, Solomon, Isaiah, and Jonah — fill his speeches.

He is master of the language peculiar to rabbis and uses it in debates. As an example, he silences the scribes and Pharisees by using their own interpretation of the Messianic psalm 110 (109): "The Lord said to my Lord, take your seat at my right hand."[84]

The Semitic style

The way he talks follows the Jewish literary texts. His phrases are often composed in the metrical pattern (common in Hebrew poetry) of parallelism in all its forms. We cite just a few examples.

[84] Cf. Mark 12:35-37; Matt. 22:41-46.

SIMPLE PARALLELISM

Disciple is not superior to teacher,
nor slave to master . . . [85]

Also

The cup that I shall drink you shall drink,
and with the baptism with which I shall be baptized
you shall be baptized. [86]

ANTITHETICAL PARALLELISM

In the same way
a sound tree produces good fruit
but a rotten tree bad fruit.
A sound tree cannot bear bad fruit,
nor a rotten tree bear good fruit. [87]

STROPHIC PARALLELISM

Therefore, everyone who listens to these words of mine
and acts on them

[85] Matt. 10:24.
[86] Mark 10:39.
[87] Matt. 7:17-18.

will be like a sensible man who built
his house on rock.
Rain came down, floods rose,
gales blew
and hurled themselves against that house,
And it did not fall:
it was founded on rock.
But everyone who listens to these words of mine
and does not act on them
will be like a stupid man who built his
house on sand.
Rain came down, floods rose, gales blew
and struck that house,
and it fell;
and what a fall it had![88]

The "heart"

The heart of Jesus is the heart of a Jew. He feels he has been purposely sent to his land for spreading love to his people: "I was sent only to the lost sheep of the House of Israel."[89] The destiny of the apostles was going to his land

[88] Matt. 7:24-27.
[89] Matt. 15:24.

and his people. On their first mission they are given precise instructions: "Do not make your way to gentile territory, and do not enter any Samaritan town; go instead to the lost sheep of the House of Israel."[90]

We have already seen him moved to tears thinking about the future end of the city of David.[91]

A man of his times

Jesus is a pious Jew who honors the traditions of his nation. Every Saturday, like everybody else, he attends the synagogue. Every year he celebrates Passover according to the approved ritual. And, like everybody else, he pays taxes for the upkeep of the temple: "When they reached Capernaum, the collectors of the half-shekel came to Peter and said, 'Does your master not pay the half-shekel?' 'Yes,' he replied, and went into the house."[92]

Now and then, someone calls Jesus a political revolutionary or a social agitator; but the evidence proves this false. He is an integral part of his society and culture, not of the modern counterculture.

[90] Matt. 10:5-6.
[91] Cf. Luke 19:41-42.
[92] Cf. Matt. 17:24-25.

He respects every law, even the requirement that priests act as health authorities certifying cures involving leprosy: "Go and show yourselves to the priests."[93] And he does not act as the administrator of simple justice for someone trying to draw him into a dispute: " 'Master, tell my brother to give me a share of our inheritance.' Then Jesus said to him, 'My friend, who appointed me your judge, or the arbitrator of your claims?' "[94]

His adaptation is so complete that he stays out of a dispute over the Roman presence in the Jewish territory. Indeed, he recognizes the right of an invader to collect taxes and impose its currency on the conquered.[95]

The financial problem

Contrary to what some have said, as a good Jew Jesus does not demonize money. He respects it and wants his mission to have a sound financial base.

His little community has a regularly appointed treasurer.[96] Some of his followers give him financial support:

[93] Cf. Luke 17:14.
[94] Luke 12:13-14.
[95] Cf. Mark 12:13-17.
[96] Cf. John 12:6; 13:29.

"With him went the Twelve, as well as certain women who had been cured of evil spirits and ailments: Mary surnamed Magdalene, from whom seven demons had gone out; Joanna, the wife of Herod's chief steward Chuza; Susanna; and many others who provided for them out of their own resources."[97]

Heaven's reward

Jesus thinks like a Jew even when speaking about the spiritual life and his bond with the Creator.

He looks upon gain (even of things beyond this world) as an incentive to do good: "Your reward will be great in heaven."[98] He takes the trouble to inform us that the living and true God is not a follower of Kantian ethics. Therefore, Jesus does not believe that indifference is necessary for good moral conduct: "And your Father who sees all that is done in secret will reward you."[99]

[97] Luke 8:1-3.
[98] Cf. Matt. 5:2; Luke 6:23.
[99] Cf. Matt. 6:4, 17.

Chapter Three

≈

Christ's Originality

Jesus is perfectly placed in Palestinian life and society. As a pious Jew, he knows the culture and history of his people. Like many teachers of Israel, Jesus is a learned rabbi who discusses, debates, and cites Holy Scripture.[100]

And yet, his presence, attitude, and teaching suddenly appear like an explosion. He is an original without precedence or equal: "No one has ever spoken like this man!" say the guards of the Sanhedrin who are sent to arrest him.[101]

Even at the start of his public ministry, his listeners believe they are in the presence of something new and unexpected. They are frightened and intimidated. The outburst at Capernaum is a good example. Mark writes of

[100] Cf. John 3:10.
[101] John 7:46.

it in frank and simple language: "The people were so astonished they started asking one another what it all meant, saying, 'Here is a teaching that is new, with authority behind it.' "[102]

The surprising miracles of the Lord are surely important here. But we will not discuss them. Our purpose is to show how new and dynamic the young prophet of Nazareth was to his listeners. His teaching differs sharply from that of the scribes.

The scribes limit themselves to analyzing the sacred texts. They decipher them and adhere strictly to the fine points. Jesus reveals the truth to everyone seeking it: "This text is being fulfilled today even while you are listening," he tells them in the synagogue at Nazareth.[103]

Political incorrectness

In the course of his ministry, even the heritage of truth securely held by Israel takes on another meaning. This unique teacher spreads a message never before heard. It casts doubts on many people's convictions and challenges the status quo. Jesus is filled with the light revealed to

[102] Mark 1:27.
[103] Cf. Luke 4:21.

Abraham, Moses, David, and the prophets. He is loyal to the Judaism practiced in the synagogue. Yet Christ often appears to be a nonconformist. To borrow a term in vogue, Jesus is politically incorrect. His political incorrectness shows when challenging commonly held ideas, alarming and confusing his listeners.

Jesus is politically incorrect when confronting tax collectors, the rich, people collaborating with the occupiers (the Roman government), and notorious thieves and prostitutes.

Of course, Jesus always condemns immorality. He pays no attention to anyone shocked and angered by his charges. In fact, his words are bold and provocative: "In truth I tell you, tax collectors and prostitutes are making their way into the kingdom of God before you."[104]

Primacy of the interior world

Jesus refuses to approve of harsh and unfair pharisaic laws and rituals. Instead, he says that what matters are good intentions and spiritual purity. In light of this, he rejects the distinction between clean and unclean foods. (The edibility of certain animals is outlined in Leviticus.)

[104] Cf. Matt. 21:31.

41

In his opinion, man can eat all animals, in conformity with God's original design.

The Gospels record how religious leaders react to Jesus' taking heretical positions:

> He called the people to him and said, "Listen and understand. What goes into the mouth does not make anyone unclean. It is what comes out of the mouth that makes someone unclean." Then the disciples came to him and said, "Do you know that the Pharisees were shocked when they heard what you said?"[105]

But on this point, he doesn't cave in or compromise. Jesus explains what he means to his followers when they are in the house:

> He said to them . . . "Don't you understand? Can't you see that nothing that goes into someone from the outside can make that person unclean, because it goes not into the heart but into the stomach and passes into the sewer?" (Thus, he pronounced all foods clean.) And he went on: "It

[105] Matt. 15:10-12.

is what comes out of someone that makes that person unclean. For it is from within, from the heart, that evil intentions emerge: fornications, theft, murder, adultery, avarice, malice, deceit, indecency, envy, slander, pride, and folly. All these evil things come from within and make a person unclean."[106]

Poverty as a blessing

Jesus is also politically incorrect when, contrary to Israelite beliefs, he says that great wealth is more a risk than a blessing. From a spiritual context, the condition of the poor is considered a privilege.[107] His disciples are amazed:

Then Jesus said to his disciples, "In truth I tell you, it is hard for someone rich to enter the kingdom of Heaven. Yes, I tell you again, it is easier for a camel to pass through the eye of a needle than for someone rich to enter the kingdom of Heaven." When the disciples heard this, they were astonished. "Who

[106] Mark 7:18-23.
[107] Cf. Matt. 5:3; Luke 6:20-25.

can be saved, then?" they said. Jesus gazed at them. "By human resources," he told them, "this is impossible; for God, everything is possible."[108]

The condemnation of divorce

Divorce was permitted and commonly practiced in Greece, Rome, and all the ancient societies. It was even accepted by Israelis, although in rabbinical schools, granting a divorce depended upon the reasons given for the request. On this point, there was often disagreement.

Speaking against Mosaic Law, Jesus boldly declares, "Whoever divorces his wife and marries another is guilty of adultery against her. And if a woman divorces her husband and marries another, she is guilty of adultery too."[109]

Jesus clarifies the contract's sacredness with a warning to the abandoned spouse who did not wish for the breakup: "Anyone who marries a divorced woman commits adultery."[110]

Reacting to the paradox of Christ's politically incorrect statement, the disciples mockingly reply, "If that is

[108] Matt. 19:23-26.
[109] Mark 10:11-12.
[110] Matt. 5:32.

how things are between husband and wife, it is advisable not to marry."[111]

Celibacy for the kingdom of heaven

Listening to the Lord's response must have confused them. But their sarcastic remarks fail to silence him. Jesus continues to speak out against the way chastity was defined by Jew and non-Jew. "But he replied, 'It is not for everyone who can accept what I have said, but only those to whom it is granted. There are eunuchs born so from their mother's womb, there are eunuchs made so by human agency, and there are eunuchs who have made themselves so for the sake of the kingdom of Heaven. Let anyone accept this who can."[112]

Never was someone so at odds with the majority opinion in Israel.

The secret font of Jesus' originality

Where does the light and energy of Jesus and his new ways of thinking originate? What hidden font refreshes and bolsters him, helps frame his decisions and

[111] Matt. 19:10.
[112] Matt. 19:11-12.

makes the "teacher of Israel" what he is? What unifies the transforming words and actions of Christ? What places them at the service of truth's authority? While remaining faithful to ancient revelation, his words shock and astound us.

As we have seen, exploring Christ's psychology leads us to his most jealous secret. Our inquiry will attempt to give us a careful and guided look into what the holy writers thought.

One obvious and immediate result of this investigation, and what the Gospels tell us, is that the heart and core of Jesus is his strong sense of the Father.

God as Father to Israel

Spiritually, Jews believed in God as a father. You may recall how the prophet Hosea touchingly described Yahweh's paternal care of Israel:

> *When Israel was a child, I loved him*
> *And I called my son out of Egypt . . .*
> *I myself taught Ephraim to walk,*
> *I myself took them by the arm, . . .*
> *I was leading them with human ties,*
> *with leading-strings of love,*

> *that, with them, I was like someone*
> *lifting an infant to his cheek,*
> *and that I bent down to feed him.* [113]

Here, the paternity of God is accepted as a bond with the elect. "For I am a Father to Israel," the Creator affirms in the prophetic texts.[114] At times, he has reason to complain: "But if I am indeed father, where is the honor that is due me?"[115]

"Son of God" is also the monarch, who by his kingly consecration, symbolizes and represents the entire nation of Israel: "He will cry out, 'You are my father, my God, and rock of my salvation.' "[116]

It is natural to believe from this that the God of Israel is "father of orphans and defender of widows" and that "like a father he has pity for his children" and for "those who fear him."[117] One also gains a personal perspective from which a just person can boast "of having God for a father."[118]

[113] Cf. Hos. 11:1-4.
[114] Jer. 31:9.
[115] Mal. 1:6.
[116] Cf. Ps. 89:26.
[117] Ps. 68:5; 103:13.
[118] Cf. Wisd. 2:16.

The Man Christ Jesus

Intimacy with the Father

Jesus proved God's paternity more movingly and clearly than anyone else in Israel. A warm and affectionate feeling for the Father marks every moment of Christ's earthly life. There is not a page of Gospel writing that does not confirm this fact. "Did you not know that I must be in my father's house?" is the first phrase of Jesus handed down to us through the scriptures. The last is: "Father, into your hands I commit my spirit."[119] Both phrases are about the Father and his design of salvation.

Whenever speaking to the Father through prayer, Jesus always looks for a silent place away from the daily rush of his ministry. He prays when he is baptized in the Jordan River.[120] He prays before helping the unfortunates brought to him.[121] He prays all night before choosing his disciples.[122] He prays at length at the conclusion of the Last Supper.[123] He prays preparing for the shocking trial of his Passion.[124]

[119] Luke 2:49; 23:46.

[120] Cf. Luke 3:21.

[121] Cf. Mark 7:34, 9:29; John 11:41; Matt. 14:19.

[122] Cf. Luke 6:12-15.

[123] Cf. John 17:1-26.

[124] Cf. Matt. 26:36-42; Mark 14:32-39; Luke 22:39-46.

Jesus' prayer

What does he say to the Father? The prayers of Jesus are well structured:

• *Adoration and praise:* "I bless you, Father, Lord of heaven and earth."[125]

• *Thanksgiving:* "Father I thank you for hearing my prayer."[126]

• *Supplication for divine glory:* "Father, glorify your name."[127]

• *Praying for his friends:* "Keep those you have given me true to your name."[128]

• *Praying for his enemies:* "Father, forgive them; they do not know what they are doing."[129]

Jesus never repents. He never seeks a pardon. There is none of the inner turmoil, fear, and trembling one feels in

[125] Cf. Matt. 11:25.
[126] Cf. John 11:41.
[127] Cf. John 12:28.
[128] Cf. John 17:11.
[129] Cf. Luke 23:34.

the presence of the holy, transcendent, and eternal Father. The state of repentance, for example, is expressed in the vision of the prophet Isaiah: "Woe is me! I am lost, for I am a man of unclean lips";[130] there is no trace of this in the prayer of Jesus.

Enriched solitude

We can, then, understand why Jesus calmly challenges the most educated people and so many widely accepted traditions. God's communion with his son gives Jesus the strength and insight to take unpopular, even solitary positions.

Indeed, the Gospels note how easily he accepts being alone, especially when choosing not to be influenced by opposing opinions: "[He] fled back to the hills alone."[131] On the other hand, his solitude is never solitude: "And yet I am not alone, because the Father is with me."[132]

Filial obedience

Conforming to the Father and his will is what Jesus really desires. It sustains him and gives him strength: "My

[130] Isa. 6:5.
[131] Cf. John 6:15.
[132] John 16:32; cf. John 8:16-29.

food is to do the will of the one who sent me and to complete his work."[133]

To do the will of God is not always easy and painless, not even for Jesus. This is dramatically revealed in the agony in the garden of Gethsemane: " 'My Father,' he said, 'if it is possible, let this cup pass me by. Nevertheless, let it be as you, not I, would have it.' "[134]

The author of the letter to the Hebrews gives this already impressive episode further testimony. Although not entirely unexpected, it offers something that may surprise us: "During his life on earth he offered up prayer and entreaty, with loud cries and with tears, to the one who had the power to save from death, and, winning a hearing by his reverence, he learned obedience, Son though he was, through his sufferings."[135]

"Yes, Father."[136] This word, *yes*, spoken by Jesus is perhaps the best description of his inner world and the secret source of much of what he said and did. St. Paul probably does not intend to say anything else when he

[133] John 4:34.
[134] Matt. 26:39.
[135] Cf. Heb. 5:7-8.
[136] Matt. 11:26.

writes, "Jesus Christ . . . was never yes-and-no; his nature is all yes."[137]

A Creator who loves

From Judaism we accept the doctrine: the God of Israel, the origin of all things, is our Father. Above all, he is the Creator who loves the work of his hands. "The Father himself loves you."[138] The Lord leaves his disciples with this simple and extraordinary truth. It is almost his legacy.

Out of love, the God of Jesus cares for all his creation, including the birds of the air and the flowers in the fields. However they act, he loves and takes care of the children of Adam with great tolerance: "so that you may be children of your Father in Heaven, for he causes his sun to rise on the bad as well as the good, and sends rain to fall on the upright and the wicked alike."[139]

In his first letter, St. John finds the right formula to express in the best way possible the theological vision of his Master: "God is love."[140]

[137] 2 Cor. 1:20.
[138] John 16:27.
[139] Cf. Matt. 5:45.
[140] 1 John 4:8.

Commandment of love

Children should resemble the Father. This ideal vision of God inspires our life: "You must be perfect as your heavenly Father is perfect."[141] Obviously, it is an impossible demand to meet. But it is a powerful way of saying that our actions, like those of God, must also be inspired by love.

Therefore Jesus teaches, "Be compassionate just as your Father is compassionate," a thought he advances to make a more extreme recommendation: "I give you a new commandment: love one another."[142]

Above all, acts of love should receive love in return. The love of the Father for his children seeks and demands the love of his children. Here, and not in rites and laws, is the substance of religion.

Therefore, it is not surprising that Jesus gets to the heart of what the God of Israel demands: " 'Master, which is the greatest commandment of the Law?' Jesus said to him, 'You must love the Lord your God with all your heart, with all your soul, and with all your mind. This is

[141] Matt. 5:48. Citation is a literal translation from the original text.

[142] Cf. Luke 6:36; cf. John 13:34.

the greatest and the first commandment. The second one resembles it: You must love your neighbor as yourself. On these two commandments hang the whole Law, and the Prophets too.' "[143]

The end of state religion

Providing another perspective, Jesus taught that citizens of one country are not given special consideration. Challenging the attitudes of his fellow citizens gives him another chance to be politically incorrect. A powerful example of this is in the synagogue at Nazareth. Jesus deliberately chooses some provocative facts from Jewish history: "There were many widows in Israel, I can assure you, in Elijah's day when heaven remained shut for three years and six months and a great famine raged throughout the land, but Elijah was not sent to any one of these: he was sent to a widow at Zarephath, a town in Sidonia. And in the prophet Elisha's time many were suffering from virulent skin diseases in Israel, but none of these was cured — only Naaman the Syrian.' When they heard this, everyone in the synagogue was enraged."[144]

[143] Matt. 22:36-40.
[144] Luke 4:25-28.

Christ's Originality

Unique in all religious history

No one has affirmed the universal paternity of God with more power and intensity than Jesus. He tirelessly brings "your Father," "your Father in heaven," your heavenly Father," "your Father who sees in secret" to the attention of his listeners. It is the central truth of his teaching.

No one with greater knowledge has pointed to love as the spirit, the sense, and the high point of our bond with God. Love is the spiritual attitude that must rule every human society. No man before him had so effectively underscored the dominance of the heart in our lives.

That should be enough to persuade us that Christianity has been a stirring voice and a revolutionary ideal within the history of religion.

Still, we haven't grasped the main reason for Jesus' originality. What inside him shapes his identity? We still do not understand his special psychology. The key to understanding his spiritual dominance for two thousand years has not yet been given to us.

True sonship

What makes Jesus of Nazareth unique? He believes that he is part of a special relationship with the God of Israel that is true only for him. If Jesus is able to think of the

Creator of heaven and earth as a father, it is because he sees himself as his son, sharing his full glory.

God, he continuously repeats, is "my Father." His every sentiment, word, and act is inspired and dominated by a conviction beyond our understanding.

The others are "his brothers." They are sometimes referred to as "sons of God" or "the least of my brothers."[145] He is especially pleased to call his disciples "brothers": "Go and find my brothers," he says to Mary Magdalene.[146] But their relationship to "sonship" and his are not identical.

He never says, "our Father" except when suggesting a prayer to others: "So, then, you should pray like this: Our Father . . ."[147] In the mysterious light of Easter morning, his language about the Father is particularly precise: "I am ascending to my Father and your Father."[148]

An unconditional originality

Throughout the Gospels, when Christ talks about God the Father he means "his" Father and "our" Father. On

[145] Cf. Matt. 25:40.
[146] Cf. John 20:17.
[147] Matt. 6:9.
[148] Cf. John 20:17.

this subject, all the Evangelists agree. So on a purely historical basis, it is hard to think otherwise. One can believe or not believe.

But no one can doubt that Jesus of Nazareth is convincing as the Son of the God of Israel in a way unknowable to others.

No man, none of history's great teachers or founders of religions, has ever had a comparable thought. Jesus is the only one.

Total relevance to the Father

Within this original vision, Jesus says that his greatness and uniqueness apply only to him. It is what he alone receives from the Father.

This helps to explain a common characteristic of Christ's preaching: Jesus continually speaks about himself. He even says things that would be offensive coming from others. Yet he is never arrogant or conceited.

No one before Jesus ever dared to say, "So if anyone declares himself for me in the presence of human beings, I will declare myself for him in the presence of my Father in heaven. [149] Or even, "No one who prefers father or mother

[149] Matt. 10:32-33.

to me is worthy of me. No one who prefers son or daughter to me is worthy of me."[150]

If taken alone, these are troubling statements. However, they are perfectly consistent with the mind of someone knowing who he is, "the only Son of the Father."[151]

[150] Matt. 10:37.
[151] Cf. John 1:14.

Conclusion

We have outlined a profile of Jesus of Nazareth. Guided by all available data, our description follows the evidence. As a result, we are able to show the strengths and weaknesses of this narrow research. The humanity of Christ has begun to emerge — at least we hope — from historical documents largely overlooked in Church teaching and other studies. This more complete picture helps us to know him better. But gaps remain in our knowledge of Jesus. Our profile should also advance our understanding of Jesus, and the friendship and affection we feel toward him. The psalm tells us he is "the most beautiful of all men."[152]

After using the most reliable sources for this careful analysis, mistakes about Christ, even those expressed by the Church, would be revealed. Accordingly, our inquiry

---

[152] Cf. Ps. 45:2.

seeks to get a better grasp of Jesus as we celebrate the second millennium. We must proceed objectively and not rely on what we think or on personal beliefs.

We lack the knowledge to reach salvation by learning Christ's mystery. It requires help from above and access to God's own intelligence because "no one can know the Son except the Father."[153] Therefore, this logical and rational discourse will proceed, opening up to the light of faith:

- *Peter's act of faith:* "You are the Christ, the Son of the living God."[154]

- *Paul's act of faith:* "[He] was handed over to death for our sins and raised to life for our justification."[155]

- *The act of faith of the four Evangelists places a crown on the entire catechesis:* "You are my Lord and my God."[156]

Our examination, now theological, will consider Jesus of Nazareth, Messiah, Risen One, only Savior of us all, Lord of the Universe, one with the Father: "true God from true God."

[153] Cf. Matt. 11:27.
[154] Cf. Matt. 16:16.
[155] Cf. Rom. 4:25.
[156] Cf. John 20:28.

Part Two

The Man Christ Jesus
by the Light of Faith

Our exploration — or better yet, our loving consideration — of Jesus' mystifying and extraordinary humanity now takes on a much different look. We intend to go beyond the reports of those who knew him during his earthly life. Believers and nonbelievers can know as much through historical reasoning. Aided by scripture, we shall seek to know the depth of Christ's mystery: who he is, who he is for us and for our salvation, and who he is for the entire living universe.

For such an inquiry, the natural light of reason will no longer suffice. We have to use the superior light of faith, a sharing of God's knowledge. Jesus himself warned us of this when he said, "No one knows the Son except the Father."[157] Therefore, ours will be a discourse among believers, although we shall also use reason and examine the positions of nonbelievers. The three topics for consideration are, respectively, the Son of the living God, the Savior, and the Head.

[157] Matt. 11:27.

Chapter Four

Christ the Son of God

We begin by reciting a famous episode in his life according to the narration of Matthew:

> When Jesus came to the region of Caesarea Philippi he put this question to his disciples: "Who do people say the Son of Man is?" And they said, "Some say John the Baptist, some Elijah, and others Jeremiah or one of the prophets." "But you," he said, "who do you say I am?" Then Simon Peter spoke up and said, "You are the Christ, the Son of the living God." Jesus replied, "Simon, son of Jonah, you are a blessed man! Because it was no human agency that revealed this to you but my Father in heaven."[158]

[158] Matt. 16:13-17.

The Man Christ Jesus

From this brief exchange, we discover what Jesus has in mind. Here he states the problem of Christ. Note how his inquiry has two parts:

• Who do the people say I am? What are the world's opinions of me?

• And you — who do you say I am? You who are my Church and carry my message through Peter — what do you tell people of me?

Even persons of faith first listen to people and then to the Church. The "people" — that is, the outside-the-Church world we encounter every day, in books, in the media, and in daily conversation — have powerful and steady influences on us for our entire lives.

Then there is the apostolic Church speaking to us from the writings of the first Christian community. The apostolic Church, its faith, is the standard for the Church today and forever. It is indelibly written upon us through Baptism.

We shall examine these opposing thoughts because the wall between the world and the Church has an exterior and an interior side. Both pierce our hearts.

Let us briefly contrast outside-the-Church knowledge with the knowledge of Christ's Church. Only from within the Church can we solve the mystery of Jesus of Nazareth. Worldly knowledge is not enough. The Father must reveal it to the faithful.

Who do the people say Jesus Christ is?

Listening to people's opinions, we learn nothing about Christ. There is no certainty among them, only many different ideas.

To clarify things, we shall arrange these opinions into three groups and review each one:[159]

• For many, Jesus is only a *myth*. He is like Orpheus in ancient Greece or Santa Claus in modern times. Jesus never lived but still enriches our lives. Or, he is a *legendary man*; although never existing, he has appeared divine. Or, if you wish, he is a *divine idea*, a faith, and a spiritual movement assuming a man's identity. To some, Jesus is a great but fictional superhuman.

• Others say Jesus is a *man* — extraordinary, but just a man. With exceptional charm, vast intelligence, and a

[159] It is worth noting that the people's judgments of Jesus are positive and loving: no one, or nearly no one, speaks ill of him.

strong personality, he changed the course of history in the universe. Jesus was simply a genius.

Some say he is a *religious genius* who discovered through intuition the fatherhood of God, worship, the creed (in spirit and truth), and the law of charity. Or *a philosophical genius* revealing the importance of the individual conscience and the dominance of the interior over the exterior world. Or *a social genius* affirming the fundamental equality among men and exalting the search for justice. Or *a political genius* looking to liberate mankind from injustice and oppression. In short, he is a man of true but not supernatural greatness.

• Jesus, says a third opinion, is a man who existed but is unknowable with *any certainty*. All our documents speak of Christ as an object of faith, love, and adoration by a primitive community. But these documents do not clarify who the Jesus of history was.

In short, he is an unsolvable enigma of history.

Proving or disproving these opinions is long but not difficult work. In a strict sense, Christians must do so to live their faith. But we do not propose it here. Our inquiry is a reflection among believers. It compares and contrasts Church positions with those of "outsiders" to illustrate the two diverse ways of approaching the mystery of Christ and their total incompatibility. It examines — hoping to end it — the coexistence in our souls between the "world" and the "Church," between the opinions of the people and the knowledge given to us by the Father. With this, we hope to grow in faith and understanding.

These diverse opinions have one thing in common about Jesus of Nazareth: they all say he's one of the prophets.

Is he a myth? History is full of myths.

Is he an idea that has influenced human events? He could be comparable to the spiritual truth of the ancient world or to Marxism of the modern world.

A religious genius? We can put him with Buddha, Moses, or Mohammed.

A philosopher? Plato and Aristotle could accept him in their company.

A social examiner? He could be classified with Marx and the French writers of the eighteenth century.

An agitator? Similar but more effective: Spartacus, Bakunin, or Thomas Paine.

A liberator? We can place him with Simón Bolívar and Giuseppe Garibaldi.

A man we cannot know about with any certainty? There are other examples: Homer, Pythagoras, and Socrates.

The Man Christ Jesus

Those trying to know Jesus of Nazareth relying solely on their own best judgment, usually reduce him to something classifiable and well known. In this way, he is no longer unique and no longer a problem.

Who do you say that I am?

Although the people's views are varied, the Church has a unified position. There is one voice in the Church with respect to Jesus Christ: the response of Peter is everyone's answer. Being faithful permits Church membership. Those who believe differently are no longer in the Church. On this point, the apostolic community does not compromise.

"If anyone comes to you bringing a different doctrine, you must not receive him into your house or even give him a greeting."[160]

"I put you on guard of the beasts in the form of a man, whom you should not only not welcome, but if possible, not even meet. You must pray for their conversion, though it be very difficult."[161]

---

[160] 2 John 10.

[161] Ignatius of Antioch (d. c. 107; disciple of John the Evangelist, bishop, and martyr), *To the Smyrnaeans* IV, 1.

Also: "They are rabid dogs that bite while hidden. You must be on your guard. They are difficult to cure."[162]

As we have shown, while worldly opinion focuses on the positions of Jesus of Nazareth, the Church faith expressed by Peter emphasizes Christ's importance: Jesus of Nazareth is "the Christ," the Son of the Living One, the Son of God." Jesus of Nazareth is beyond comparison.

But how is the uniqueness of Jesus expressed? Is Jesus unclassifiable?

Still a living presence in the world today, the apostolic Church, speaking through Peter, talks of his uniqueness in three ways: messianism, the resurrection from death, and divinity.

Messianism

For Jews, the "messiah" at the time of Christ would represent every hope of Israel: He would have reestablished the kingdom of David, renewed and purified the cult of God, made known the will of Yahweh and his design of salvation, and ended their history of pain and humiliation.

It is interesting to note that the messiah did not imply any special uniqueness. The Jews recognized many messiahs

[162] Ignatius of Antioch, *To the Ephesians* VII, 1.

in their past: David, the kings, the priests, and the prophets had, from time to time, been given this name. This recalls for us the ritual of anointing with oil.

But even in the future, the Jews do not necessarily expect a Messiah to be a single person. The writings found at Qumran and *The Testaments of the Twelve Patriarchs* report that certain religious societies were waiting for more than one messiah in the latter days. Besides David as messiah with kingly rights, there was also the expectation of Aaron as messiah invested with priestly dignity.

Even the promise of Moses found in Deuteronomy seems to have stirred up expectations of a prophet different from the messiah-king and messiah-priest: "Yahweh your God will raise up a prophet like me; you will listen to him."[163] We can trace an echo of this citation in the questioning put to John the Baptist: "Are you the prophet?"[164]

Jesus only reluctantly accepts being called messiah. But in the last week of his earthly life, he seems to say that all the messianic expectations are fulfilled in him. After the anointing at Bethany, he plans to enter Jerusalem as king and Davidic Messiah. He does what prophets do

[163] Deut. 18:15.
[164] John 1:21.

(such as the expulsion of sellers from the Temple porticos and the cursing of the fig tree). Recalling Melchisedek, he acts as priestly messiah with the bread and wine at the Last Supper. In his Passion, he confirms the messianism of the suffering Servant of Yahweh, of whom Deutero-Isaiah had spoken. By concluding with the apparitions and the ascensions, he reveals himself as the Son of man, the end-of-the-world messiah. As prophesied in Daniel, Jesus comes in the glory of God and places the seals on human history.

We don't wonder, then, at seeing the apostolic Church continually presenting Jesus of Nazareth as the Christ and only messiah. He fulfills all the aspirations of men.

"Jesus is the Christ" is among the most frequently documented confessions of faith in the Acts of the Apostles.[165] Although largely accepted in Judaism, it was also widely proposed to all believers (even to the non-Jews). The name *Christ* in the Greek-language communities becomes a component of the name *Jesus*. At Antioch — a non-Jewish community — the word *Christian* originated to identify the disciples of Jesus of Nazareth: "It was at Antioch that the disciples were first called Christians."[166]

[165] Cf. Acts 2:36; 3:20; 5:42; 9:22; 17:3; 18:5, 28.
[166] Cf. Acts 11:26.

The Man Christ Jesus

The contemporary Church still offers the faith of Peter to all: Jesus is the Messiah. He is the divine response to the basic expectations of men. All the eternal aspirations that burn in human hearts — truth, certainty, liberty, goodness, and joy — are uniquely fulfilled in Jesus of Nazareth.

The conclusion is evident: the uniqueness of Jesus — Jesus the unique one, waited for by man, and Jesus the unique one, sent by the Father — rules out any confusion over his identity. If Jesus is the Messiah, we need not seek any other man more important in human history. Human greatness is defined in this light. The Messiah has already come: no ideologue, no liberator, no exceptional personality is able to charm and hold the truly Christian heart. As St. Ambrose[167] said: "The Church already has its enchanter."

Thus, in the light of Christ and his unique messianism, the Christian is able to justly evaluate each new spirit, person, or doctrine that comes on the scene.

The Resurrection

Peter's declaration, calling Jesus the Son of the Living One, will dominate apostolic preaching following the

[167] St. Ambrose (c. 340-397), Bishop of Milan.

Pentecost: the Son of the Living One does not remain a prisoner of death and corruption. "You [have] killed," says Peter, "the prince of life. God, however, raised him from the dead, and to that fact we are witnesses."[168]

Therefore, the second element of Christ's uniqueness is he's alive. There is no doubt about this. The paschal announcement "He has risen" (which is the starting point of Christian faith) says that Jesus of Nazareth, a man who died on the Cross two thousand years ago, is today physically alive. He is alive in body — not in his message, his example, his positive influence on human history, not in the poor, in the brothers and sisters, or in the community. All are true reflections of Christ, glorious and decisive in Church matters. But all depend on the truth of his rising and being physically alive.

This event, which makes Jesus of Nazareth unclassifiable and unequaled, also makes a case for those accepting this announcement.

It is important for the Christian to understand that:

• Here is the reason for the deepest division among men: "But they had some argument or other with

[168] Acts 3:14-15.

him about their own religion and about a dead man called Jesus whom Paul alleged to be alive."[169]

• This opinion makes the believers seem absurd to the nonbelievers: "Here we are, fools for Christ's sake."[170]

• There cannot be an intermediate position between those who say today that Jesus is physically alive and those who say he is physically dead; there is no compromise between believers and nonbelievers.

• If Christ is risen, everything is changed for man: death, the final act, has been conquered and no longer has the last word.

• This is what makes Jesus of Nazareth truly revolutionary: after dying, he continues to be physically alive.

The divinity

Peter proclaims, "You are the Son of God." We have here the third and most important, but mystifying, part of the uniqueness of Jesus of Nazareth: his divinity. It was historically

[169] Cf. Acts 25:19.
[170] 1 Cor. 4:10.

unthinkable within the Jewish culture, rigid and fiercely monotheistic, that a divine man could be born from a woman. Influenced and moved by the light of the Resurrection, the apostolic Church arrived at this shocking belief. "My Lord and my God"[171] is the profession of faith by the disbelieving Thomas and the core of the Johannine doctrine.

The apostolic Church expresses this difficult faith in various ways, clarifying its many parts:

• Paul: Jesus is "of divine nature" and "for this God raised him high, and gave him the name which is above all other names."[172]

• John: Jesus is the Word that "was with God and the Word was God."[173]

• Matthew places the Son between God the Father and the Spirit of God, on the same level: "In the name of the Father and of the Son and of the Holy Spirit."[174]

[171] John 20:28.
[172] Cf. Phil. 2:6, 9.
[173] John 1:1.
[174] Matt. 28:19.

• The letter to the Hebrews: "But to the Son he says, 'Your throne, God, is forever and ever.'"[175]

• Through the paschal light, the apostolic Church learns the truth. Because of the paschal light, it has finally understood that Jesus had cautiously claimed divine rights for himself: he places himself on the same level as the Legislator of Sinai: "In truth I tell you . . .";[176] he claims for himself the right to forgive sins;[177] he considers himself the Judge of men and history; he proclaims himself the "master of the Sabbath" and greater than the Temple;[178] he says that he is the only teacher, not only always right, but "the truth";[179] he places himself above the angels;[180] he presents himself as the object of a love that must be greater than love of father, mother, wife, children, and siblings;[181] he considers

[175] Heb. 1:8.
[176] Matt. 5:18.
[177] Matt. 9:2; Luke 7:36-50.
[178] Matt. 12:6-8.
[179] John 14:6.
[180] Mark 13:27.
[181] Matt. 10:37; Luke 14:26.

himself not one of the sons of God but the only Son.[182]

In Jesus' words, God and he are on the same level: "No one knows the Son except the Father, just as no one knows the Father except the Son . . ."[183]

Jesus' declaring himself God undermines the kindly, tolerant view many scholars use to describe him. Appreciating Jesus as wise, just, and great, they never recognize him as Lord and God. This modest view of Christ is contradicted by all our evangelical documentation. A man who says what Jesus says cannot be judged wise, just, or great. He doesn't deserve our esteem and cannot be honored unless everything said of him, all that he says of himself, and all that the apostolic Church declares of him is untrue.

Therefore, no one can believe out of a general reverence for Christ. Either we reject him, or we fall on our knees before him. Jesus himself had foreseen this: "Do you suppose that I am here to bring peace on earth? No, I tell you, but rather division."[184] Luke, in the infancy narratives, writes that Jesus is placed "for the fall and for the

[182] Matt. 21:33-34.
[183] Matt. 11:27; Luke 10:22.
[184] Luke 12:51.

rise of many" and remains in the world "destined to be a sign that is opposed — so that the secret thoughts of many will be laid bare."[185]

⁓

As we have seen, Christ's problem is this: Jesus is either "one of the" or "the." Either He is classifiable or beyond classification. Either His worldly appearance is important but comparable to others, or it is unique, decisive, and not repeatable. This is the question. To be Christian is to understand that Christ is "the" without qualifications. He is the one and only.

As a result, our relationship with him is different from any other ones we have. It is a light given to us from on high: "neither flesh nor blood has revealed this to you, but my Father who is in heaven."[186] The recognition of his godhead is not a theorem's conclusion, but our yielding to the Holy Spirit: "Nobody is able to say, 'Jesus is Lord' except in the Holy Spirit."[187] Our love for him has no comparisons: "No one who prefers father or mother to

[185] Luke 2:34-35.
[186] Cf. Matt. 16:17.
[187] 1 Cor. 12:3.

me is worthy of me."[188] Focusing our life on him must be total, absolute, and complete: "Anyone who finds his life will lose it; anyone who loses his life for my sake will find it."[189]

[188] Matt. 10:37.
[189] Matt. 10:39.

Chapter Five

≋

Christ the Savior of the World

After trying to understand who Jesus is for himself, we can now consider who Jesus is for us. In truth, this second inquiry further refines and completes the first one. Our answering the question "Who is Jesus?" must clarify his role as savior.

Both infancy Gospels (Luke and Matthew) — about family remembrances and the theological meditation of the first Judeo-Christian community — present the name *Jesus* as a heavenly source offering salvation. "When the eighth day came and the child was to be circumcised, they gave him the name Jesus, the name the angel had given him before his conception."[190] And: "You must name him Jesus, because he is the one who is to save people from their sins."[191]

[190] Luke 2:21.
[191] Matt. 1:21.

The Man Christ Jesus

His is, then, a prophetic name designating his mission and in some way his nature. It has a specific meaning affirming the salvation granted us by God. *Jesus* (Hebrew: *Iehoshua*) means precisely "Yahweh saves."

Misery and man's greatness

What does *saved* mean? What is salvation? In the dictionary's definition, *saved* means having overcome every danger unharmed. Salvation means being freed from an impending evil. Obviously, total salvation is the objective of God's intervention, liberating man from the evil touching his heart and affecting his destiny.

Recalling the Pascal language, the theme of salvation reminds us of man's misery and greatness.[192] Man's misery is caused by ignorance. He is charmed and led astray by its lies as he blunders his way toward death. Prejudicial thinking and sinfulness make him unhappy.

Although man's misery is great, tragic, and inescapable, it bears witness to his nobility and uniqueness among all creatures. From the beginning, within each human heart

---

[192] The author refers to French philosopher Blaise Pascal's (1623-1662) *Thoughts on Religion and Other Subjects* (1660).

dwells a desire for truth. Thus, our mortality is made for a life without limits. Sinning does not defeat our basic hope for a more just existence.

Indeed, the human soul's greatness increases our despair. Man knows he is foolish. He knows he must die. He knows he is not innocent. This awareness sharpens the pain and makes his life more unendurable. It places him in a continuous state of prayer. Whether through words, thoughts, or sentiments, the human being cries out. With all our strength, we cry out for freedom from misery, emptiness, burdens, unimportance, sin, weakness against evil, poor health, and death.

The Church and the world

With respect to salvation, let us put a fresh gloss on the two opposing realities, the "world" and the "Church." Both precede us. Both are always outside and in some way within us, stressing us out, with their clashing points of view.

What do the people say about salvation?

Some recognize the misery of man and think it inevitable. Man's lack of intelligence will always dog him. Death is the failure of hope, our total defeat, and the sad conclusion of a senseless life. There is nothing to do about it. We are all dominated by evil, ego, sin, and laziness. Nothing can change this.

There is a great and universal need for salvation. But it will never come. Every guess is an illusion. There is no redemption for man.

Highly respected authors in Italian literature, such as Leopardi and Pirandello, brilliantly express this bitter pessimism. It usually grows over the years.

At the other extreme, many people are in conflict with themselves. They believe that man is already good, attractive, and happy. He has no need for personal redemption.

"Enlightened" and diverse "doctrines" have developed from this simple and original "dogma" dominating a large part of contemporary culture. We shall attempt to simplify and list them in a concise and easy-to-follow way:

Enlightened conservatism: Man is fine as he is. In fact, everything is going along so well that no change is necessary in his heart or the world around him.

For obvious reasons, even if no one has the courage to say it, the rich and the privileged believe this. Appearing in many disguises, it creeps into the human spirit. The only truthful one unafraid to admit his capitalistic conservatism is, perhaps, Donald Duck.

Christ the Savior of the World

Enlightened radicalism: Man is naturally good, but shackled and degraded by historical barriers and many other pointless impediments:

- from the remains of feudalism in the organization of the state;

- from the collective ties of labor;

- from the traditional and regressive vision of rationalism and science;

- from prohibitions and other intriguing taboos poisoning a person's life.

To save man from error and falsely desiring, say the radical enlightenists of the eighteenth century, he needs only to learn the Copernican theory, Darwinism, and the metric decimal system. Nothing has substantially changed from then.

To redeem man and make him happy as a modern, enlightened libertarian, he must only believe that "it is forbidden to forbid." To save man from sin, tell him that sins do not exist. At worst, man is only partly at fault. To free man from the anguish of death make him believe it's a false problem not worth considering.

The Man Christ Jesus

Enlightened Marxism: Men are naturally good, except for the dark forces of reaction. Capitalism (the seat of evil) must be eliminated and replaced with socialism. In this way, man will have justice, freedom, and happiness. These ideas are widely discredited today. Only those stuck in the past continue to believe it.

The responses to sin and death by enlightened radicals can be easily placed with Marxists.

It is interesting to reveal the parallels and direction of these three "diverse" enlightenments.

At last questions have been answered about man's nature. This includes divorce, abortion, euthanasia, homosexuality, birth control, *et cetera.*

We suspect that the only original and complete vision of man is the Christian vision. Christianity is the only event new to history.

A third group remarking on salvation put a Christian face on every position examined up to this point. Guided by evangelical beliefs, they fall into one of the following categories:

• Personally without hope, some think that faith is a consoling illusion supporting the weakest spirits.

Without help, they cannot confront "the apparent truth" of how existence is a meaningless tragedy.

• Those who put a Christian face on conservatism: the gospel is socially precious because, by offering the prospect of eternal life, it helps to end acts of vengeance and social unrest in the present life.

• Those who think that the message of Christ is one of liberty according to a populist social and political point of view see that message as a means of overcoming all binding restrictions of moral obligations.

• Those who are Christians for socialism say that class struggle gives meaning to the socially oppressed. This is the core of Church teaching.

On close observation, using a militaristic image, all are cases calling Christ to arms. In these examples, he is not seen as the realized Lord, but as a "recruit" given a uniform and banner by the "princes" of the world. Jesus Christ, then, is able, enlisted, and, usually after a brief service, discharged.

~

We conclude from these different hypotheses that "people" are confused. They think human salvation is either impossible or unnecessary. Many, however, believe that an "exterior" salvation is possible and necessary. This happens when society's social, political, and cultural conditions or structures are changed.

These theories maintain that some exterior or interior salvation is possible and necessary. All believe that man must save himself. Therefore, no intervention from above is necessary, possible, or even desirable. It is an idea, described by a former Italian statesman, as "a secular redemption or self-redemption," for those relying on their own efforts, abilities, and free will. This includes an establishment of government and the rule of law.[193]

The formula of faith

The harmonious response of Christ's apostles or Church conflicts with the secular world's multiple opinions.

Man's salvation as stated in the Gospel:

• is primarily an internal and transcending salvation — a salvation from falseness and futility, from sin and its slavery, from death, and the wickedness of earthly mortality;

[193] Translated from the Italian, *Il mondo frantumato*, by Giovanni Spadolini (Milano 1992), 387.

• is the fruit of the Father's merciful love that is assured for everyone, because "he wants everyone to be saved and reach full knowledge of the truth";[194]

• was obtained through Jesus Christ, the Son of God, crucified and raised up, and cannot be obtained from any other: "Only in him," says Peter in the first days of the Church, "is there salvation; for of all the names in the world given to men, this is the only one by which we can be saved."[195]

Because each person is individually saved, he must believe and accept the Lord Jesus with all his heart. The Father's saving grace goes directly to him.

It is taught, with clarity, by an ancient "formula of faith," stated by St. Paul: "That if you declare with your mouth that Jesus is Lord, and if you believe with your heart that God raised him from the dead, then you will be saved."[196]

[194] 1 Tim. 2:5.
[195] Acts 4:12.
[196] Rom. 10:9.

The Man Christ Jesus

Three questions about salvation

We are now asked to seek and know the truth from divine revelation. It is the first rigid theological analysis of our work. This will not be an easy task. To understand how Christ's salvation worked to the advantage of all people, we must answer three separate questions:

- What did the Lord do to bring us salvation?

- What gives these actions their redemptive value?

- How did Christ's actions effect our salvation?

They are difficult and serious questions. We must clearly formulate answers, mindful that only in the kingdom of heaven will the truth be known. Honoring our responsibility as faithful researchers, we the living can only hypothesize, knowing mistakes will be made.

The acts of salvation

With what specific acts of salvation did the Lord Jesus save us?

For centuries Church teaching made salvation the Passion and death of the Lord. A close rereading of the Gospels — the rules of our faith — teaches us to combine preaching with doctrine.

Christ the Savior of the World

The early preaching clearly indicates that the Resurrection is also an act of salvation: "It was the God of our ancestors, who raised up Jesus, whom you executed by hanging on a tree. By his own right hand God has now raised him to be leader and Savior, to give repentance and forgiveness of sins through him to Israel."[197] The two sides of the paschal mystery are, in the ancient formulas of faith, a single source of salvation: "He was handed over to death for our sins and raised to life for our justification."[198]

Furthermore, one learns from reading the Gospels that many reported miracles are not simply displays of power, but helpful signs of a saving presence among men. And Christ's words are listened to, not as clarifications of doctrine (which were the teachings of the scribes), but as "words of eternal life." The light ended the slavery of darkness. As revealed truth, it makes us free.

Clearly, his existence among men — first of every word and every act — is affirmed in the infancy Gospels as the coming of the Savior.

The prologue of the fourth Gospel sees the redemption of humanity already in progress with the coming into the

[197] Acts 5:30-31.
[198] Rom. 4:25.

world of the *Logos,* or the eternal Word of God. "The Word became flesh; he lived among us."[199]

Therefore, Jesus is all about saving: he has redeemed us not only by what he did, but also by what he said and what he is.

Also, the Gospels tell us that Christ's saving work reaches its fulfillment with his Passion, death, Resurrection, and entrance into heaven. There, he makes his sacrificial offering, "having won [for us] an eternal redemption."[200]

The salvation proof

The second question is more difficult. It makes us look deeper into the redemptive act. Christ's saving life began with the Incarnation. It ended in glory and the unknowable life of God. But why is it saving? What gives this story the power to redeem?

As a start, the great theologians and Fathers of the Church offer us two leads to the heart of this mystery. The first (originating from St. John and thoroughly examined by the Greek Fathers) emphasizes the redemptive value of the Incarnation.

[199] Cf. John 1:14.
[200] Heb. 9:12.

Christ the Savior of the World

Our theological premise departs from the belief that man's Fall and ruin was caused by the loss of contact with God's divine nature. His restoration and salvation lies in re-acquiring the living "icon" of divinity (which man possessed in God's original design) and again being a son sharing the Father's nature.

Divinely personalizing it within our history, the Word's human nature restores the ideal man in truth and substance. He now conforms to the Father's unchangeable will. It is therefore just. Entering into communion with the living God, allowed by Jesus, the new Adam accepts (through his life of knowledge, love, and grace) and reflects upon (only from a distance by participation) the mystery of having both a human and divine nature. Thus, we have man's passing from the state of injustice, enslavement to evil, and mortality, to the state of justice, spiritual liberty, and eternal life.

It must be noted that the redemptive Incarnation is not limited to the Son of God's earliest earthly life. Human nature is assumed in all its depravity and mortality (with the exception of Original Sin). The Word Incarnated increasingly shares our destiny throughout his earthly life. It includes tiredness, sadness, fear, suffering, and death.

The Man Christ Jesus

The Passion, death on the Cross, and Resurrection represent the last moment of the Incarnation. It allows man's redemption.

The second theological perspective also derives from the synoptic writings of the apostolic community and the letters of Paul. It presents the work of salvation as restoring justice denied. Man "returns," retracing the footsteps that had distanced him from God. This perspective highlights the redemption of Christ's suffering and death. It shapes the mystery of the incarnate Son of God obeying the will of the Father.

It is worth saying that in the decline and fall's darkest moment, man foolishly turned against the Creator, choosing death over life. Redemption reunites the will of man with the will of the Father. It returns him to the source of life completed in the Resurrection.

But because it is God's will that justice be respected and that righteousness be accompanied by joy and sin by sorrow, the man who "returns" must accept suffering as necessary to restore his damaged will cut off from God. Accepting suffering and death with his fellow sinners, Jesus complies with his Father's justice. Obediently, the human will is divinely remodeled. It turns away from corruption and ruin.

Christ the Savior of the World

Let us note that these two perspectives do not exclude one another. Rather, they are integrated. Together, they lead us toward a deeper knowledge of God's plan. A complete understanding of God's purpose, in all its beauty, will be given us only when we have gone beyond our earthly existence. Only then shall we have the open vision of the Redeemer and the Father's eternal design of salvation.

Our original connection with Christ

The third question is at the center of the entire mystery. How is it that what Christ did has brought us salvation? It is as if the older brother endured the injections that cured the younger brother of pneumonia.

With its customary presentation of redemption as the "satisfaction of a debt," the Latin Church[201] has not felt the urgency and gravity of this problem. Christ is said to have paid in our place. We know that whoever pays the debt liberates the debtor from his obligations.

But as soon as this image is subjected to conceptual analysis, its shortcomings are immediately revealed. To

---

[201] The Latin Church refers to the western or Roman Catholic Church.

whom is the debt paid? To the Devil, as some ancient writers would wish? But can one speak of the right of the Devil? To God? But what Father would demand this bloody payment from his innocent son? If treated as a moral debt, how can Jesus pay for what others owe?

The answer is found in understanding that it is not so much a "vicarious satisfaction" (an idea commonly used by Latin theology for this inquiry), as much as a mysterious "solidarity between Christ and us": what he has fulfilled is to our advantage.

The solution must recognize the link between Christ and humanity. Its closeness almost makes Jesus and all mankind a unique living organism. The link is not so much the fruit of redemptive sacrifice (which we have always thought is the connection making the Church the Mystical Body of Christ), but the one reason the sacrifice of Jesus can be truly redemptive for us. This link with humanity did not occur in some moment of world history but was there when the universe began.

The mystery of the redemption worked for us by Jesus of Nazareth, crucified and raised up, naturally affirms an eternal accord. From all eternity, God made Christ the source and the model to which all aspire. From the beginning, Jesus was predestined to be the summit, head, and sum of all things. The Creator willed everything into existence, modeled after and closely connected to Christ.

The intervening sin did not break up the substance of God's design. Indeed, in a way, it confirms and verifies it because the Son of God is not separated from his guilty brothers and sisters. Rather, he remains the healthy head of a sick organism. Christ becomes for humanity the source of healing and new life.

This truth has decisive and incalculable consequences for our vision of man, the world, and our time in it. We shall consider this as our next topic. We can summarize our discussion with a few observations:

• There is a vast distance between man's view and the Christian truth about salvation: they are incomparable. Confusion affects our thinking. Therefore, a Christian's first duty is to think clearly and stop believing in false idols. "What can light and darkness have in common. How can Christ come to an agreement with Beliar [Satan] and what sharing can there be between a believer and an unbeliever?"[202]

[202] 2 Cor. 6:14-15.

The Man Christ Jesus

• Evangelical salvation does not look at man's flaws. It looks at man in his purest state. Salvation is given to us with the light of truth, the infusion of charity — the new and true capacity to love — the remission of sins, confronting evil with freedom, a sharing of the divine nature, the victory over death through resurrection and eternal life.

Saying salvation only causes social, political, and cultural change goes against the teaching of the apostolic Church. It is also contrary to the Lord's work and inconsistent with Christianity itself.

The Son of God was not born just to set up the International Red Cross or any other worthy service organizations. The Word profoundly touches everything. The Incarnation, Passion, death, Resurrection, and Pentecost have already conquered the world. They changed reality and renewed man's fate. We are already the new world.

• It is up to us to bring the good news into our lives. It is up to us to free ourselves from the old ways of worldly behavior and walk into a new life.

We still struggle for social justice, civil liberties, and the establishment of a more brotherly and humane society. This is not because these are the goals of Christ's redemption, but because injustice, oppression, cruelty, and alienation clash with the Christian message. They darken and contradict it. "So for anyone who is in Christ, there is a new creation: the old order is gone and a new being is there to see."[203]

[203] 2 Cor. 5:17.

≈

Chapter Six

Christ the Head of the Body

At this point, we have shown that world views are incompatible with Peter speaking through the Father's revelation. We have spiritually cleansed our conscience of hidden cultural idols that change and distort the truth about Christ and salvation. Now our spirits will try to understand the effects that accepting Jesus of Nazareth — the only Lord and Savior — will have on our life and earthly obligations.

To best accomplish this, let us summarize everything learned about him through divine revelation.

He is the Messiah. Therefore, he comes to us through God's mystery. He fulfills our needs, overcomes our doubts, and responds to our endless questions.

He is the Living One. Rising up, he has opened a crack in death's barrier, the cruel obstacle to our life's journey. In its place, he has offered us hope. We can look forward without fear.

The Man Christ Jesus

He is the Son of the Eternal One. By assuming our nature, he has restored us to the dignity of God's living image and likeness. He has forever joined a physical humanity, still subject to the forces of evil, to the blessed and elusive truth of divinity.

He is the perfect Man, holding and interpreting in himself all humanity. By saying yes to the Father's will and need for justice, proven by his heroic death on the Cross, he has overcome the no of Adam's rebellion.

With this in mind, each of us must say, "I feel called, drawn, and connected with Jesus of Nazareth, crucified and raised up. If he is the Messiah, he is the Messiah for me; if he is the Lord, he is my Lord; if he is the Savior, it concerns my salvation. I am not a spectator to the business of others; I am the party involved."

But the revelation of Christ, and the uniqueness of his saving grace, tells me that everyone benefits as much as I. If he is unique, his salvation is universal. If no one else saves, all must be saved in him. If he is the only one finding the truth in people and renewing them, then all must be receptive. They are connected to him. He unifies them. In our eyes, if he is the one giving meaning and consistency to life, then everything apart from him is diminished. Everything separated from him is stained, corrupted, and lost.

St. Paul expresses this fundamental concept of the Christian vision, using the image of the "head." Christ is the "head" of the Church. Even before, he is the "head" of the universe.[204]

Lastly, we shall examine "Christ the head" and some of its consequences.

Christ, the head of the Church and the universe

Crucified and raised up in the heavenly sanctuary, Jesus of Nazareth continuously offers his redemptive sacrifice to the Father. Through the same action, he pours his spirit out on the world and promotes the truth of the Church.

Therefore, Pentecost is not just an episode in the history of the apostles on the fiftieth day after the Resurrection of the Lord. It never stops being active. We are continually exposed to the aftershocks caused by the Lord's presence at the right hand of the Father.

From the pierced and glorified human heart of Jesus, the Spirit gushes forth like an endless spring. It irrigates the earth and makes it productive. It empowers fragile and imperfect creatures to be instruments more effective

[204] Col. 1:18.

in the service of the new life. It touches souls and makes them divine.

Thus, the sacredness and the sanctity of the Church come to life. The "sacred" effect:

• Despite personal confusion, weak and ordinary men make Christ's mission everlasting. Through the centuries, apostolic succession ensured that bishops succeeded bishops. Every earthly dynasty eventually ends.

• Human writings, often inelegant, ungrammatical, and tied to a culture, express God's eternal word. They are offered to us as Sacred Scripture.

• Simple and humble things such as water, oil, bread, and wine become in the sacraments signs of the presence and sacrifice of Christ surrounded by followers.

But the Spirit sent by the crucified and risen Christ also empowers the invisible world inside — the minds, hearts, and consciences. This is the sanctifying effect.

Therefore, man senses the gift of illumination. It gives him an understanding of the divine truth. Even when it seems difficult and remote, the gift of inspiration moves him to resist temptation, give up old vices, or perform a good deed that taxes his abilities.

He who surrenders to this sweeping tide by living the faith and being inspired by charity becomes a temple of the Holy Spirit. He receives, like an unexpected gift from the Lord, this mysterious and hard-working Host. Dwelling within him, it is the source and foundation of the life of grace.

These are the wonders of "godliness." Even though man is born a fallen and troubled sinner, the Spirit of Christ secretly flourishes in him. Thus, all the "sacredness" and "sanctity" existing under heaven by this perennial Pentecost — gathered and united in one being — is the unfailing and forever-young miracle of the Church.

In light of these considerations, the Church can be understood like all humanity. This is according to the Father's eternal design. Through the Holy Spirit, it is reached, purified, renewed, and unified by the crucified and risen Savior now living in divine glory.

The Church is a living unity; Christ is the "head." In the words of St. Paul, the church is the "body" of Christ; "He is the Head, the Body, that is, he is the Church."[205]

[205] Col. 1:18.

The Man Christ Jesus

Whoever accepts the word of Jesus has been marked by his sacraments. He participates in faith with the same knowledge Christ has of God and other things. He has in his heart the same love for the Father and his brothers and sisters. He hosts in his soul (inner sanctuary) the same spirit that proceeds from him. That person is included among the living members of this body. To grow in the Church means to draw closer to Christ, to become more like him, and to share in the divine life.

Christ is the head of the created universe

Reflecting on the mystery of salvation, we sense that there was a connection between men and Christ even before any church relationship — a fruit of the Redemption. Indeed, before the universe began, there was a connection between all creation and Christ. Although continually attacked by Satan, it has never been lost.

Everything from the beginning was created and designed for man. All things, therefore, are placed at the service of man. All things find in man a conscience and a voice to praise God. All things exist as if lesser participants of the gift of life contained in human nature.

Such a human-centered vision is clearly expressed by St. Ambrose: "He finished the sixth day and concluded the creation of the world with his masterpiece, man, exercising dominion over all living beings. He is the culmination of the universe and the most beautiful of every created being."[206]

However, from eternity all men have been conceived in the image of Christ the Redeemer, modeled on him from the beginning, finalized in him, completely connected to him.

Even before being head of the Church, Christ is head of the created universe. Each man belongs to him even before he is reached and transformed by his Spirit. Every man resembles him in some way even before participating in his divine life.

Belonging to Christ is different from belonging to the Church:

• because it is original and has no need for a single act or a community to sustain it;

• because it is universal and belongs, not only to the baptized and faithful, but to everyone;

[206] "... *in quo principatus est animantium universarum et summa quaedam universitatis et omnis mundanae gratia creaturae*" (St. Ambrose [c. 340-397; Bishop of Milan], *Exameron*, VI, 10, 75).

• because it is permanent: not even man's rebellious behavior could change his true nature. Although born faded and defiled, he is an image of the Lord.

Man's first contact in this world with Christ is flawed. It aspires to be fulfilled and exalted by redemption. Like the rough sketch of a painting, it needs to be completed before becoming a masterpiece. But the rough draft is enough and already contains everything. No amount of damage can destroy it. Each thing, each man, then, is born deeply marked by the Lord.

However, each thing, each man is also born under the "reign" of the demon ("death came to reign over all," says Paul[207]), impeding from conception his even anticipating the possession — or yet, the gift — of divine life. This is the mystery of Original Sin. The redeemed life (or baptismal life, or Church life, or life of grace) liberates man from the suffocating oppression of evil. This verifies his nature as a "living icon of Christ." Increasingly, it causes him to grow in connection and likeness with his Savior.

As we have shown, the man who faithfully lives his Christian life truly becomes "more man." He fully realizes

[207] Rom. 5:17.

the original and indestructible nature of "image." Man always strives to become an ever more "similar image."[208]

During the apostolic era, the Christian community joyfully spoke about Christianity and its fundamental truth. This was summarized in a hymn by St. Paul in his letter to the Colossians:

> *He is the image of the unseen God,*
> *the firstborn of all creation*
> > *for in him*
> *were created all things*
> *in heaven and on earth:*
> *everything visible and everything invisible,*
> *thrones, ruling forces, sovereignties, powers —*
> *all things were created through him and for him.*
> *He exists before all things*
> *and in him all things hold together,*
> *and he is the Head of the Body,*
> *that is, the Church.*
> *He is the Beginning,*
> *the firstborn from the dead,*
> *so that he should be supreme in every way;*

[208] Cf. Gen. 1:26.

> because God wanted all fullness to be found
>   in him
> and through him to reconcile all things to him,
> everything in heaven and everything on earth,
> by making peace through his death on the
>   Cross.[209]

⁓

The truth of the primacy of Christ in the Church and throughout the created universe carries with it some important consequences for the Christian vision of reality.

• *Each man is an "icon" (image) of Christ.* Each man — whatever his convictions, his actions, or his state of mind — is a primitive image of Christ. He is always lovable in the clear eyes of faith.

For this reason, Christianity has no requirement to love the believer, but to love one's "neighbor," even if the neighbor lacks spirituality. It is enough for Christians that one is a man and an "icon of Christ."

Naturally, it is wrong to say that anyone in Christ's image is corrupt, imperfect, faithless, and evil. Therefore, he

[209] Col. 1:15-20.

who loves the Lord tries to be more like him. Every Christian must be apostle and evangelizer.

• *Every earthly value reverberates with the richness of Christ.* If the richness of creation is gathered in Christ, then he is truth, beauty, and holiness. Every true value encountered on earth is, then, a reflection of his light. Every true value is, then, innately Christian.

In nature, in history, in research and invention, in the expression of art and in contemplation, all truth, all beauty, all the good given to us, if it truly concerns the true, the beautiful, and the good, comes from the Word Incarnated. Without diminishing himself, he continuously shows himself wherever a creature of God exists.

To respect, honor, and love values — wherever they are found and whatever form they take — can also be, if the heart is pure, a subconsciously real way of belonging to Christ.

On the other hand, to possess Christ in faith, to know the source, the summit, the fullness of every truth, every beauty, and every justice, means to find oneself in the privileged state of living a life of values. He is better than one who sees and expresses them without knowing Christ.

The Man Christ Jesus

• *The example of Christ:* Just as all the world's values are already in some way "Christian," all that exists in Christ has value.

And because the Christ we speak of is the Son of God, crucified and raised up according to the Father's plan, and because he is the beginning and creator of men and the universe, whatever is a part of him has value, even as much as it may appear valueless to human reason. Some examples are suffering, failure, defeat, and death.

These are judged valueless by non-Christian reason not yet a part of real existence, assuming real existence finds its center, model, and justification in the sacrificed and glorious Christ.

But reason, enlightened by faith, knows the importance and greatness of the crucified and risen Lord. Being "fully" and "totally" reason, it reverses the logical process. Non-values such as suffering, failure, defeat, and death, if lived by Christ, become values for us.

Presented here are the premises underlying the Christian solution to the mystery of human suffering.

Two sides, one order of things

A clear distinction exists between where all things and all men are naturally placed (caused by Adam's fall) and the redeemed condition (coming from Christ's sacrifice and the ensuing release of the Spirit).

These conditions exist in Christ, through Christ, and for Christ (as expressed by the hymn in the letter to the Colossians). Is one able, then, to speak of things outside the Church?

Yes, if we mean that things have form and are in a natural state continuing to exist. They are rationally attainable even when desecrated by sin and wounded in their original state, or when they are touched and renewed by the transforming action of the Spirit. For example, man continues to be man even when rebelling against God's design. This alienates him from Christ. He remains a man even when becoming a living member of the Church body.

No, not if we mean that things in the natural order exist independently from Christ and can be understood without reference to him. In any case, like it or not, he remains their Head and Lord. Indeed, Christ (who alone gives meaning to this universe and to man in particular), can be known only through faith. Total comprehension of Christ and all creation is given only to those who recognize through faith the highest order of thinking.

Certainly, we do not live in a world of shadows. Things really exist. Every creature has a reason to be. Each one has its own physical appearance, its own particular nature, and therefore its own meaning. Creatures are not empty opportunities offered to God's power. They have a secondary but real purpose.

But this does not mean that the world is a jumble of separate, different, and independent fragments. The revelation of Christ, around whom all things are planned, tells us that a unifying design exists. Everything exists as part of a living structure finding its head in Christ.

If this is true, nothing is adequately known when uprooted from the whole. Every creature's knowledge is always an abstract knowledge. No creature has a partial existence. All live, at least at first, according to a plan and within a community.

Therefore, if it is true that every human science has properly respected methods and forms, it is also true that no science excluding knowledge of Christ fully explains its subject. Even if we cannot quote Jesus to answer every question, disobeying the Lord Jesus decreases the power we have over the universe.

"All belong to you, but you belong to Christ and Christ belongs to God."[210] All things are ours only if we belong to

[210] 1 Cor. 3:23.

Christ. If the lordship of Christ is not perfectly recognized, we are defeated by forces rebelling against us.

"In fact, the materialistic civilization," says John Paul II, "in spite of humanistic declarations accepts the primacy of things over a person."[211]

• *True knowledge of man comes from Christ.* If man is always a youthful image of Christ, each true and honest study of man is also a study of Christ.

Any decent person thinking about man and loving him knows a little of the mystery of the God-Man. This love is objectively directed toward the Lord Jesus, even if he does not know it: "For I was hungry and you gave me food."[212]

On the other hand, if it is true that man was modeled on Christ and not Christ on man, then none of history's important studies allows us to truly understand the mystery of man.

Only Christ and those to whom he has been revealed by the Father in heaven know who man is. Being the perfect and ideal man, Christ alone knows man.

[211] *Dives in Misericordia*, n. 11.
[212] Matt. 25:35.

The Man Christ Jesus

For this reason, every humanistic philosophy that disregards Christ (or worse, is against the Christian faith), gives life to a cruel and dehumanized society. With unequaled clarity and reach, the twentieth century involuntarily taught us this tragic lesson.

Conclusion

In the brief space of this book, we have attempted to draw closer to Christ. We are well aware that he is a Christian mystery, a reality that transcends us. For this reason, he has the power to save us. Each of us has a need to be saved.

We have attempted to approach Christ's mystery, to see and respect its uniqueness. We have concluded that lowering Christ to our level, or to the level of our interests (social, cultural, economic, political), trivializes him. It makes him meaningless and useless.

We have attempted to understand how his absolute uniqueness gives him an important and universal relevance. No people or cultures can ignore him without being dehumanized. No person can consciously be apart from Jesus without losing himself as a person. No time is greater than the time when Christ lived, no matter what others believe. Jesus is not an extravagance, an option, or just a novel idea. His presence or his absence (our acceptance or refusal) touches our soul and determines our fate.

He is the Lord and asks to be part of our life, our thoughts, and our decisions. Our mind is filled with this memory; our will is guided by this obedience; our humanity cannot be fully alive unless it grows in communion with him.

He is the Lord of the universe, and he cannot be excluded from any part of it.

He is the Lord, even if he does not impose himself upon us. Instead, he freely offers himself for our acceptance.

Our joy that he exists conquers any possible sadness. The eyes that followed him in faith can no longer look with sorrow at the world and its history. The heart staying open to him is open to all creation. It no longer withdraws into its own despair.

Because he exists, we are a saved people. Because he exists, we are a Church. Because he exists, all things must be renewed: every thought of Christ must give way to a new humanity in Christ.

Giacomo Cardinal Biffi

Cardinal Giacomo Biffi was born in 1928 in Milan, Italy, and ordained in 1950. He taught theology at seminaries in the Archdiocese of Milan, served as parish priest in the town of Legnano, and was then transferred to the parish of St. Andrea, where he created the first parochial pastoral council.

In 1975 Pope Paul VI appointed him titular bishop to Cardinal Giovanni Colombo, Archbishop of Milan. He received episcopal ordination in 1976 and was named archbishop of Bologna in 1984. The following year, he was elevated to cardinal by Pope John Paul II. In the Roman Curia he served on the Congregations for the Evangelization of Peoples, the Clergy, and Catholic Education.

Cardinal Biffi is the author of numerous theological and catechetical publications and is Archbishop emeritus of Bologna.

Sophia Institute

Sophia Institute is a nonprofit institution that seeks to nurture the spiritual, moral, and cultural life of souls and to spread the Gospel of Christ in conformity with the authentic teachings of the Roman Catholic Church.

Sophia Institute Press fulfills this mission by offering translations, reprints, and new publications that afford readers a rich source of the enduring wisdom of mankind.

Sophia Institute also operates two popular online Catholic resources: CrisisMagazine.com and CatholicExchange.com.

Crisis Magazine provides insightful cultural analysis that arms readers with the arguments necessary for navigating the ideological and theological minefields of the day. *Catholic Exchange* provides world news from a Catholic perspective as well as daily devotionals and articles that will help you to grow in holiness and live a life consistent with the teachings of the Church.

In 2013, Sophia Institute launched Sophia Institute for Teachers to renew and rebuild Catholic culture through service to Catholic education. With the goal of nurturing the spiritual, moral, and cultural life of souls, and an abiding respect for the role and work of teachers, we strive to provide materials and programs that are at once enlightening to the mind and ennobling to the heart; faithful and complete, as well as useful and practical.

Sophia Institute gratefully recognizes the Solidarity Association for preserving and encouraging the growth of our apostolate over the course of many years. Without their generous and timely support, this book would not be in your hands.

www.SophiaInstitute.com
www.CatholicExchange.com
www.CrisisMagazine.com
www.SophiaInstituteforTeachers.org

Sophia Institute Press® is a registered trademark of Sophia Institute. Sophia Institute is a tax-exempt institution as defined by the Internal Revenue Code, Section 501(c)(3). Tax I.D. 22-2548708.